WORLD HISTORY BY ERA

The Age of Revolution

VOLUME 6

Other titles in the
World History by Era series:

WORLD HISTORY BY ERA

The Age of Revolution

VOLUME 6

Stuart A. Kallen, *Book Editor*

Daniel Leone, *President*
Bonnie Szumski, *Publisher*
Scott Barbour, *Managing Editor*

Greenhaven Press, Inc., San Diego, California

Every effort has been made to trace the owners of copyrighted material. The articles in this volume may have been edited for content, length, and/or reading level. The titles have been changed to enhance the editorial purpose.

Library of Congress Cataloging-in-Publication Data

The Age of Revolution / Stuart A. Kallen, book editor.
   p. cm. — (World history by era; vol. 6)
  Includes bibliographical references and index.
  ISBN 0-7377-0703-8 (pbk. : alk. paper) —
ISBN 0-7377-0704-6 (lib. : alk. paper)
   1. History, Modern—18th century. 2. History, Modern—19th century. 3. Revolutions—History—18th century. 4. Revolutions—History—19th century. 5. United States—History—Revolution, 1775–1783. 6. United States—History—1783–1865. I. Kallen, Stuart A., 1955–   II. Series.

D286 .A35 2002
909.7—dc21
                                2001023579
                                        CIP

Cover inset photo credits (from left):
Corel Professional Photos; Photodisc; Corel Professional Photos; Corel Professional Photos; Planet Art; Digital Stock; Photodisc
Main cover photo credit: Giraudon/Bridgeman Art Library
Dover, 43
Library of Congress, 127, 139, 152, 190
North Wind Picture Archives, 20, 86
Prints Old and Rare, 108, 201

Printed in the USA

CONTENTS

Chapter 2: 1787–1799

revolutions on both sides of the Atlantic in the last quarter of the eighteenth century.

Chapter 3: 1800–1812

Chapter 4: 1813–1827

Chapter 5: 1828–1837

FOREWORD

T he late 1980s were a time of dramatic events worldwide. Tragedies such as the explosions of the space shuttle *Challenger* and the Chernobyl nuclear power plant shocked the world out of its complacent belief that humankind had mastered nature and firmly controlled its technological creations. In U.S. politics, scandal rocked the White House when several high-ranking officials in the Ronald Reagan administration were convicted of selling arms to Iran and aiding the Nicaraguan contra rebels. In global politics, U.S. president Ronald Reagan and Soviet president Mikhail Gorbachev signed a landmark treaty banning intermediate-range nuclear forces, marking the beginning of an era of arms control. In several parts of the world—including Beijing, China, the West Bank and Gaza Strip, and several nations of Eastern Europe—people rose up to resist oppressive governments, with varying degrees of success. In American culture, crack cocaine and inner-city poverty contributed to the development of a new and controversial music genre: gangsta rap.

Many of these events were unrelated to one another except for the fact that they occurred at about the same time. Others were linked to global developments. Greenhaven Press's World History by Era series provides students with a unique tool for examining global history in a way that allows them to appreciate the seemingly random occurrences as well as the general trends of human progress. This series divides world history—from the time of ancient Greece and Rome to the end of the second millennium—into ten discrete periods. Each volume then presents a collection of both primary and secondary documents that describe the major events of the period in chronological order. This structure provides students with a snapshot of events occurring simultaneously in all parts of the world. The reader can then see the connections between events in far-flung corners of the world. For example, the Palestinian uprising (*intifada*) of December 1987 was near in time—if not in character and location—to similar

protests in Beijing, China; Berlin, Germany; Prague, Czechoslo-
vakia; and Bucharest, Romania. While these events were different in many ways, they all involved ordinary citizens striving for
self-autonomy and democracy against governments that were attempting to impose strict controls on their civil liberties. By making the connections between these events, students can see that
they comprised a global movement for democracy and human
rights that profoundly impacted social and political systems
worldwide.

Each volume in this series offers features to enhance students'
understanding of the era of world history under discussion. An
introductory essay provides an overview of the period, supplying essential context for the readings that follow. An anno-
tated table of contents highlights the main point of each selection. A more in-depth introduction precedes each document,
placing it in its particular historical context and offering bio-
graphical information about the author. A thorough chronology
and index allow students to quickly reference specific events
and dates. Finally, a bibliography opens up additional avenues
of research. These features help to make the World History by
Era series an extremely valuable tool for students researching
the rise and fall of civilizations, social and political revolutions,
cultural movements, scientific and technological advancements,
and other events that mark the unfolding of human history
throughout the world.

INTRODUCTION

he era between 1775 and 1848 has been called the Age of Revolution by historians, and for good reason. It was a time like no other, when the dictates of kings were swept aside by average citizens turned revolutionaries who believed that governments should be run for the good of "the common man."

In concrete terms this widespread revolutionary fervor caused such earth-shattering events as the expulsion of the British monarchy from the American colonies and the beheading of a French king. Fallout from these two events alone resulted in wars and bloody revolts in nearly every nation in Europe, South America, and elsewhere.

It was no accident that this happened in the last quarter of the eighteenth century. The earlier part of the 1700s was known as the Enlightenment. It was a period when great philosophers such as Voltaire, Jean-Jacques Rousseau, and others achieved fame for their insightful criticism of Europe's despotic kings, such as France's Louis XIV, who ruled with absolute dictatorial power.

In *The Age of Ideas*, George R. Havens explains the power wielded by the philosophers:

> Seldom has literature been forged into a more potent weapon in the slow battle for progress. These were authors who never forgot that the war on behalf of the unknown future must be won or lost first of all in men's minds.
>
> In an age of repression and censorship, the ablest writers of the day learned to beat the government's game with wit, allegory, clever fiction, or surreptitious publication. The general public, in turn, eagerly patronized the contraband peddlers of forbidden books or manuscripts.[1]

The philosophers promoted strong beliefs in human reason, self-expression, and the basic rights of liberty and justice. They also called on average citizens to question widely accepted religious dogma and pursue scientific and artistic reasoning in everyday life. As German philosopher Immanuel Kant once said, "Dare to know! Have the courage to use your intelligence."[2]

REVOLUTIONARY WORDS

Although the European philosophers believed in the power of their words, few expected to see their ideas carried out. The kings of Europe, who also ruled the lands of the New World, were too rich and powerful to voluntarily turn the reins of government over to the common people. Indeed, no precedent existed for such an event—it had never happened before in history.

The unique situation in the American colonies, however, provided fertile ground for putting the philosophers' words into action. Separated from the mother country by the vast Atlantic Ocean and located in a seemingly endless landmass filled with limitless natural resources, American colonists already experienced a much greater degree of freedom than their European counterparts.

The American Revolution was ostensibly about paying taxes to King George III without having representatives in Parliament, the British governing body. But it was also a forum on the separation of church and state, the sovereignty of the American people, and effective checks and balances in government. And it took place in a land without an established king, hereditary nobility, or nationally recognized church. In *Revolution and Romanticism*, Howard Mumford Jones explains:

> Except in the lamentable matter of slavery . . . [the] governing idea was not merely that men are born free— that was an old concept—but also that they are entitled not merely to individual liberty but to equality and happiness. Happiness was supposed to spring not alone from freedom and equality but also from three other important theories of the century: the physiocratic theory, which . . . held that an [agricultural] nation was likely to be contented; the laissez-faire theory, which held that [business regulation] was wrong and that contentment would be increased if government interfered as little as possible with trade and manufacture; and the utilitarian theory, which held that happiness was possible here and now and need not be postponed to heaven. It argued that individual fulfillment arose from a surplus of pleasure over pain, a doctrine which in turn required men to live amicably together.[3]

By the 1770s such beliefs, stated simply as "life, liberty, and the pursuit of happiness," were widely established in the American colonies. They were debated in printed essays, letters, books, newspaper articles, pamphlets, and elsewhere. In some areas of the country, such as Boston, Philadelphia, and New York City, it seemed that almost everyone, from the humblest farmer to the wealthiest businessman, had something to say about what were called the natural rights of man.

When American colonists started the American Revolution in 1775 by firing on British soldiers at Concord, Massachusetts, the

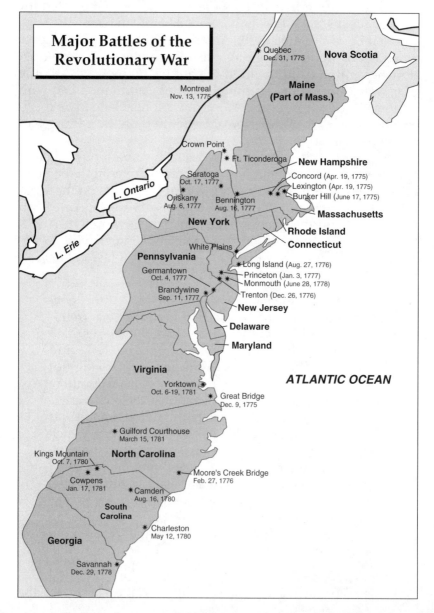

Major Battles of the Revolutionary War

initial volleys of gunfire were indeed "the shots heard round the world." While the war had many causes, the ideas of life, liberty, and happiness were soon to shake the royal foundations in palaces from Paris to St. Petersburg.

THE REVOLUTIONARY TIDE

Since France and England had been bitter enemies for centuries, the French sent men and money to America to help the revolutionaries defeat the British in 1783. Unfortunately, the $240 million that King Louis XVI lent the Americans for their quest nearly bankrupted the French treasury. These financial difficulties quickly caused Louis to regret his generosity toward the Americans. Indeed, French citizens could not help but notice that their king was financing Americans who were rebelling against a government much less repressive than their own.

By 1788 France was teetering on the verge of dire economic collapse. The desperate king called leading nobles, clergymen, and average citizens to his palace at Versailles to form a governing body—called the Estates General—to advise him on the national crisis. It was the first time this assembly had been organized since 1614, and the body voted to give equal powers to the clergy, nobility, and representatives of the middle class, who were known as the Third Estate. Meanwhile, in the months before the Estates General met, Louis was struck another blow when France experienced one of the worst harvests in its history. Citizens rioted in the street, clamoring for bread as widespread starvation swept across the countryside.

When the Estates General finally did meet in June 1789, the commons, composed mainly of middle-class merchants, took control of the assembly. Never before had a royal government put so much power in the hands of average citizens. They named themselves the National Assembly and demanded civil rights such as trial by jury, privacy of the mail, drastically reduced taxes, and reform of royal law.

Afraid of losing his power, Louis ordered the Royal Guard to make a show of force on the streets of Paris. Meanwhile, the poorest citizens of Paris began to riot and soon formed their own army, the National Guard, to protect and defend the National Assembly. News of the revolution spread through the countryside, and before long angry peasants were storming the lush homes of the nobility, burning records of debts and taxes owed, and occasionally, the houses themselves.

In August the National Assembly, renamed the Constitutional Assembly, created a document called the Declaration of the Rights of Man and Citizen, much like the Declaration of Independence created by Thomas Jefferson. The document called for the creation of a constitutional monarchy in which the nobility would keep their property but lose their rights of taxation.

Louis withheld his support of the declaration and remained at the lush Palace of Versailles. During a banquet, however, twenty thousand hungry peasants stormed the palace and ordered the royal family back to Paris. Louis had no choice but to be escorted back to the city by thousands of armed peasants.

THE DEATH OF A KING

When not at work, the National Assembly divided itself into clubs with differing political beliefs. One of the most influential was the Jacobin Club, made up of middle-class professionals, one of whom was a lawyer named Maximilien Robespierre. The Jacobin Club believed that its ideals of liberty at any cost could save France. They became very popular, and Jacobin clubs formed in cities all across France. Before long, the Jacobins were the most powerful faction in the French Revolution.

Although the new assembly began reforms in education and government, the country continued to face the problem of bankruptcy. In a sweeping move to gain considerable wealth, the government seized the huge landholdings of the Catholic Church. This paid off the national debt, but it angered many in the strongly religious regions of southern France.

The kings of Prussia and Austria were alarmed that the French Revolution might spread beyond its borders and envelop their countries. In the summer of 1792, an allied army of Austrians and Prussians invaded France with the intention of restoring royal authority to Louis. A hastily assembled revolutionary army, however, turned back the Austrian invaders. A new assembly was called, which outlawed the monarchy.

In November charges were made that Louis XVI had planned the previous summer's Austrian invasion to restore his power. The king was put on trial for treason, was found guilty, and was executed. His queen, Marie-Antoinette, met the same fate.

THE REIGN OF TERROR

Emboldened by their new power, the National Assembly, now known as the National Convention, declared that France should expand its borders throughout Europe. It declared war on Britain, Holland, and Spain. The ill-trained revolutionary armies invaded neighboring countries, but they were quickly subdued. Embarrassed, the National Convention ordered the conscription of 650,000 men into the army.

France was now at war, and any opposition was considered

treason. The government set up dozens of revolutionary tribunals in major cities to find traitors. The committees filled the jails with people suspected of counterrevolutionary activities. As the terror increased, the term *traitor* was applied to almost anyone who spoke out against the government madness. Led by Robespierre, the Jacobins, who held the most power, began to execute their opponents in the National Convention. With those enemies gone, the Jacobins turned on one another; those who had helped Robespierre gain power were also executed. Within a year 35,000 people lost their heads to the guillotine. In Paris alone, during one seven-week period 1,376 people were beheaded.

In 1794, when Robespierre demanded yet another purge of enemies, he, too, went to the guillotine. The Reign of Terror was over, and a new group, called the Thermidorians, took the reigns of power. The nobility who had survived the Reign of Terror held a majority in this new government, and many revolutionary laws were repealed. A young general by the name of Napoléon Bonaparte turned the government's guns on the hostile mobs protesting in the streets. In the following years Napoléon led the French armies on campaigns across Austria, Italy, Egypt, and elsewhere.

In 1799 the Jacobins were driven from assembly chambers by Napoléon's troops, and the French Revolution was over. Within weeks Napoléon had gained control of the government. In 1804 General Napoléon named himself emperor of France, and once again the country was ruled by a single man.

REMAKING EUROPE

While Napoléon was busy creating a royal court from his statesmen and generals, he was also developing ambitious plans to rule the Western world. In 1805 Napoléon's newly formed Grand Army invaded Germany and Austria, destroying both the Austrian and Russian armies that had assembled to fight the French. In 1806 and 1807 Napoléon annexed several states that made up the present-day countries of Italy and Germany while his armies conquered Poland, defeated Prussia, and marched into Spain.

The emperor's luck began to turn in 1812, when the Grand Army attempted to conquer Russia but was driven back by extremely frigid winter weather. The next year Prussia, Russia, Britain, and Sweden banded together, and during the next several years Napoléon and his increasingly battered army was driven out of every country on the continent. By 1815 Napoléon's empire was gone, and the former emperor was exiled to St. Helena, an isolated island in the South Atlantic, twelve hundred miles off the coast of Africa.

Thousands of French citizens were imprisoned and sentenced to death by guillotine during the Reign of Terror.

After defeating Napoléon, the victors organized the Congress of Vienna to redraw the map of Europe. In an unprecedented meeting of kings, emperors, and viscounts from Britain, Austria, Russia, and Prussia, attempts were made to restore pre-Napoléon dynasties across the continent.

The wealthy nobles divided up Europe as if it were a jigsaw puzzle. Prussia was given almost half of the German state of Saxony, along with the Rhineland and Westphalia; Russia was given a large section of Poland; Belgium was handed over to the Netherlands; and Lombardy and Venice, several regions of present-day Italy, were turned over to Austria. The country of Germany was created from a loose confederation of states; Norway was ceded to Sweden; and the former kings of Spain, Portugal, and Italy were returned to their thrones. Hoping to put a lid on the democratic ideas of the French Revolution, which had already spread into other countries, Louis XVIII, brother of Louis XVI, was crowned king of France.

Although the monarchy was restored for a time, many of Napoléon's revolutionary ideas of governance were retained. Under the emperor, the French government had become a streamlined, centralized, and efficient bureaucracy. This modern form of administration replaced old-style royal government even as the kings remained in power. And Napoléon's Civil Code, the basic rule of law, was used as the foundation for new legal systems in Holland, Belgium, Italy, and elsewhere. Although the kings were once again the rulers of the continent, the major changes brought by Napoléon and the French Revolution were now an indispensable part of nineteenth-century Europe.

THE WAR OF 1812

In the meantime, on the other side of the Atlantic, the United States experienced problems of its own. Although Great Britain had been fighting Napoléon's armies in Europe, it still found the money and manpower to fight a separate battle, the War of 1812, against its old enemy, the United States.

In a sense this war was revenge for the American Revolution, which had never quite ended for the British in 1783. Although a peace treaty had been signed, Great Britain had never withdrawn its troops from the Great Lakes region, and the English continued to agitate Native Americans to fight American settlers in the Northwest Territory (the present-day states of the Ohio, Indiana, and Illinois) and elsewhere.

The hostilities leading to the War of 1812 were exacerbated during the French revolutionary wars and the Napoléonic Wars when the United States was caught between the policies of France and England, the two most powerful nations on the earth. In 1807 a decree known as the British Orders in Council ordered all neutral trade to continental Europe be first inspected in Great Britain. Conversely, France issued two decrees that declared Britain to be in a state of blockade and condemned neutral shipping that obeyed the British Orders in Council. With these conflicting decrees, any merchant shipping goods to Europe would be subject to hostilities from either the French or the British.

At the time Great Britain ruled the Atlantic, and it soon began seizing hundreds of American merchant ships that had little choice but to ignore the British Orders in Council. Others were subject to seizure depending on the degree of corruption exhibited by British inspectors. Likewise, to keep the pressure on the United States, the British navy began confiscating American merchant ships directly off the U.S. coast. It also instituted a practice known as impressment, which involved kidnapping American sailors and forcing them to serve in the British navy.

As the shipping industry in New England fell into economic ruin, Americans called for a war to redeem the nation's honor. As far as the mighty British government was concerned, they were ready to take back the land they had lost to a ragtag group of revolutionaries a little less than three decades earlier.

As the war began, Americans realized that their military was not ready to fight against the well-trained British army. In the first campaigns of the war, the United States was easily repelled when it attempted to invade Canada, which had remained under British sovereignty after the Revolutionary War. By August 1814 the United States faced total defeat as the British army marched into Washington, D.C., and burned the White House and other government buildings.

The tide turned against the British a short time later when a fierce naval battle on Lake Champlain destroyed the British fleet in the Great Lakes region. The war was over by the end of 1814, but little had changed between the two nations. The American public, however, was proud that their nation, barely thirty years old, had once again defeated the most powerful nation on the earth. As a surge of nationalism swept through the ever-expanding country, the postwar years became known as "the Era of Good Feelings."

JACKSONIAN DEMOCRACY AND THE TWO-PARTY SYSTEM

The War of 1812 had made a national hero out of General Andrew Jackson, who won the only U.S. land battle against the British in the Battle of New Orleans. Although Americans bragged about this victory, it was fought, ironically, weeks after the peace treaty had already been signed between Great Britain and America. Because news traveled slowly at that time, Jackson did not know that peace had been secured. Nonetheless, he came to represent the victory of the common man over seemingly insurmountable odds.

Jackson was elected to the U.S. Senate from the state of Tennessee in 1822, and he almost won the presidency in 1824. At that time, however, the United States only had one political party, and a backwoodsman such as Jackson could not wrest power from the aristocratic East Coast rulers of America. These men, such as president John Quincy Adams, believed in a laissez-faire system of government in which businessmen were free to pursue their financial goals with little concern for farmers, artisans, and other average citizens.

In 1828 the Democratic Party was formed based on the then-revolutionary concept that the common citizen should be protected against the predatory business practices of the ruling class. With the support of the Democrats, Jackson was elected president. His inauguration saw an outpouring of recent immigrants and poor, middle-class, black and white Americans to celebrate their victory.

THE REVOLUTIONS OF 1848

Americans had much to celebrate. Most shared in the prosperity that was the envy of the world. When French aristocrat Alexis de Tocqueville traveled to the United States in the 1830s, he was overwhelmed by the average citizen's dedication to the ideals of life, liberty, and the pursuit of happiness as detailed in the Declaration of Independence. While ignoring the horrors of black slavery and genocide against Native Americans, de Tocqueville wrote page after page of praise for the American system in his 1835 book *Democracy in America.* When his book became a worldwide best-seller, it inspired revolutionaries around the globe to emulate the American system.

By the 1840s Europe was ripe for another revolution in France. As in earlier years, an economic depression and three consecutive years of crop failures left the bourgeoisie and peasants in a sour mood.

Once again the revolution began in Paris. This time the liberal king, Louis Philippe, was driven from his throne. After the National Assembly, dominated by middle-class businessmen, took over the government in June 1848, a second republic, modeled on the 1789 revolutionary government, was established.

News of the second French Revolution swept across Europe. In Vienna, Austria, violent demonstrations forced Minister of Foreign Affairs Klemens von Metternich from office, more than three decades after he had redrawn the borders of Europe after the Napoléonic wars. Austria controlled Hungary, Croatia, Italy, and other republics that also demanded independence.

A tide of revolution quickly turned, however, when Austria's new emperor, Francis Joseph, called in the Russian army to suppress the uprising. Francis Joseph, who would remain emperor until World War I, also regained control of Italy, Hungary, and other Austrian satellites.

The Paris revolution had also inspired an uprising in neighboring Germany, where revolutionaries hoped to create a unified German empire. The German revolution, however, faced many insurmountable problems, as the *Oxford Illustrated History of Modern Europe* explains:

> [Everything] . . . went wrong for the revolutionaries. They were everywhere divided: liberals and radicals moved apart, to left and to right; both came to fear the peasants whose destabilizing of the German and central European countryside had done so much to paralyse the old order's power of resistance. The French . . . [second] republic was only saved by an appalling week of street-fighting in Paris . . . [at a] cost [of] 20,000 dead. After that, order reigned in Paris. . . . Meanwhile, the third reactionary power, Russia, like Britain almost untroubled in 1848, re-emerged as the policeman of eastern and central Europe . . . [with the Russian] army [cutting] the ground from under [the revolutionaries].[4]

The French Revolution ended much the same way as it had in 1789, with the country bitterly divided between rich and poor. As de Tocqueville later wrote, "Society was cut in two: Those who had nothing united in common envy; those who had anything united in common terror."[5]

The old order remained firmly entrenched. However, the second great wave of revolution did manage to change the way business was done in the palaces of Europe. The kings realized it was much easier to maintain power when they had the full support of their people, and by the end of the century most European countries were governed with some form of constitution that granted basic rights to the masses.

FROM SEA TO SHINING SEA

The United States was unscathed by the bloody revolts of the Europeans, who—nearly seventy-five years after the American Revolution—continued to fight for rights most Americans now took for granted.

As in earlier times, Americans had many advantages that their European counterparts could only dream of. Between the American Revolution and the second French Revolution, the United States had grown from thirteen states on the East Coast to a land that stretched from the Atlantic to the Pacific oceans. Americans who were unhappy with their situation could simply pick up and move west, laying claim to lands that Native Americans were increasingly forced to surrender to white settlers.

By 1848 the United States had become a country that the founding fathers would have barely recognized. Railroads and canals increasingly covered the landscape. The populations of New York, Philadelphia, Boston, and other cities had exploded, aided by wave after wave of immigrants fleeing the troubles in Europe. Smaller towns had grown out of the wilderness to become prosperous bastions of democratic values. Gold was discovered in California only three months after it had become a state, and the glittering riches on the West Coast beckoned to people across the globe.

With its democratic form of government firmly established, the United States had become a world power and the envy of repressed peoples everywhere. The dreams of eighteenth-century philosophers had become a reality. The United States, though still imperfect, had become a land where people were free to pursue their own agendas for happiness while electing their own leaders to carry out their wishes. The power of that vision set the standard for revolutionary leaders of the time, and it has continued to do so from the Age of Revolution to the twenty-first century.

NOTES

1. George R. Havens, *The Age of Ideas*. New York: Free Press, 1965, p. 9.
2. George Constable, *Winds of Revolution*. Alexandria, VA: Time-Life Books, 1990, p. 8.
3. Howard Mumford Jones, *Revolution and Romanticism*. Cambridge, MA: Harvard University Press, 1975, p. 151.
4. T.C.W. Blanning, ed., *Oxford Illustrated History of Modern Europe*. Oxford: Oxford University Press, 1996, p. 25.
5. Quoted in George Constable, ed., *The Pulse of Enterprise*. Alexandria, VA: Time-Life Books, 1990, p. 45.

WORLD HISTORY BY ERA

1774–1786

CHAPTER 1

A MIX OF INDIAN AND WHITE CULTURES

COLIN G. CALLOWAY

By the time of the Revolutionary War in 1775, the American colonies were a kaleidoscopic mix of interacting cultures. With Native Americans and white Europeans influencing each other, late eighteenth-century America was one of the most multicultural places on the earth.

As Colin G. Calloway, associate professor of history at the University of Wyoming, writes, the social revolution during which American Indians from dozens of tribes adopted the ways of French, English, Russian, Dutch, German, and other whites while Europeans moved into the wilderness to live like Indians, was as dramatic as the American Revolution.

I n the summer of 1775, as news of the opening conflicts in the American Revolution spread west, a young Englishman recently arrived from Derbyshire in search of good land traveled to the "Indian country" of the Ohio Valley. Nicholas Cresswell went with a party that consisted of two Englishmen, two Irishmen, a Welshman, two Dutchmen, two Virginians, two Marylanders, a Swede, an African, and a mulatto. On August 27, Cresswell visited a mission town of Moravian Delawares at Walhack-tap-poke or Schönbrunn, a settlement of sixty log houses covered with clapboards, arranged along neatly laid-out streets, and a meeting house with a bell and glass windows. The parson preached through an interpreter, the Indian congregation sang hymns in Delaware, and the service was conducted with "the greatest regularity, order, and decorum, I ever saw in any place of Worship in my life." Four days later, Cresswell was at the Delaware town of Coshocton, where he participated in an Indian dance. The beating of drums, the gourd rattles, the rattling of deer hooves on the knees and ankles of the male dancers, and the jingling of the women's bells struck Cresswell's ears as "the most unharmonious concert that human idea can possibly conceive," and the sight of an "Indian Conjuror" in a mask and bear skin was "frightful enough to scare the Devil."

Indian America by 1775 was a landscape of cultural polyphony, or more accurately perhaps, cultural cacophony, a country of mixed and mixing peoples. Cresswell's brief sojourn among the Delawares exposed him to some of Indian country's diversity and to its mixture of change and continuity. He saw Indians who wore European clothes but retained traditional loincloths and nose rings. He noted that they had learned to curse from Europeans, observed that white traders cheated them blind whenever they could, lamented the destructive effects of alcohol, and learned that smallpox had "made terrible havoc." He traveled with Indian girls who served as guides during the day and bedfellows at night. He witnessed Indian orators in council, and became something of an ethnographic observer. He had "been taught to look upon these beings with contempt," but instead developed "a great regard for the Indians" and felt "a most sensible regret in parting from them." Three months in a changing Indian world changed a visiting Englishman.

The next year, a New Jersey captain in Iroquois country was struck, as Cresswell had been among the Delawares, by the contrast between the quiet and orderly church services of the Oneidas, and the noise, drumming, and chanting of Seneca, Cayuga, and Onondaga ceremonies. Many Oneidas by this time were Presbyterians, although traditional beliefs and rituals survived intact. Some people were literate in both English and Iroquoian. Some Oneida children attended school, many Oneidas were skilled carpenters and farmers, and trade with Europeans was a major economic activity.

MIX OF OLD AND NEW

Other Indian communities throughout the eastern woodlands displayed similar blends of old and new. Single-family log cabins had replaced, or coexisted with, traditional wigwams and communal longhouses. At the mission village of Lorette on the Saint Lawrence, for example, the Huron Indians "built all their houses after the French fashion." In New England, Indian families who still lived in wigwams likely had their share of European-manufactured household goods, and even European-style furni-

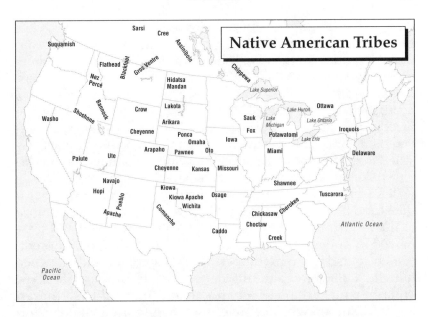

Native American Tribes

ture. The palisaded villages of the seventeenth century had often given way to more open and dispersed settlements in which kin groups settled near their fields and livestock rather than around the village council house. Indian towns sometimes comprised clusters of small hamlets; sometimes they were large multiethnic trading centers.

Indian America had always experienced changes, of course, but their tempo and impact increased dramatically after the arrival of European and African people, producing what [historian] James Merrell has aptly described as a "new world" for Native Americans. "It is strange what revolution has happened among them in less than two hundred years," remarked [eighteenth-century author] Hector De Crèvecoeur. At first contact, America was what John Winthrop called a land "full of Indians." By the end of the colonial period, the Indians of the eastern woodlands numbered perhaps 150,000 people in a world teeming with immigrants. Most who survived did so by adjusting in some measure to Europeans and their ways.

Adjusting to Indian country and Indian people also created a new world for the newcomers. Like the rest of colonial America, Indian country was an arena in which a "kaleidoscope of human encounters" generated a web of cultural exchanges as Indians, Africans, and Europeans made . . . "creative adaptations" to new places and new peoples. Those Indians, Africans, and Europeans were not representatives of monolithic groups, but individuals of different ethnicity, geography, gender, and status. "Indians" were Abenakis, Delawares, Senecas, and Cherokees; "Africans" were

Ibos, Ashantis, and Yorubas; "Europeans" were Swedes, Germans, Scots, Irish, and English—and Englishmen from London were very different than Englishmen from Cornwall or Yorkshire.

Mohawks shared their villages with individuals from other tribes, and their valley home with people of Dutch, German, Scottish, Irish, and English descent. Delawares lived alongside Swedes and Finns before Germans, Scotch-Irish and Welsh settled their lands. Franco-Indian communities and individuals persisted long after the collapse of New France. Catholic Indians often spoke French and bore French names, wearing crucifixes as well. Cosmopolitan French communities that embraced both Indians and blacks dotted the landscape from the Saint Lawrence to the mouth of the Mississippi. Non-Indians lived and trespassed in Indian country, with or without the Indians' consent. Scotch-Irish borderers competed with Cherokee and Shawnee hunters in the latter's traditional hunting territories; Cherokee and Shawnee villages were home to Scots and Irish Indian agents; adopted white captives took their place in the kinship network of Indian societies. Runaway slaves added an African strand to the fabric of southeastern Indian communities. People who intruded on Indian country often pursued their own independence from eastern authorities and rendered ineffective much of colonial and early national Indian policy.

Indian people likewise participated in shaping colonial and revolutionary American society. They served in colonial armies as soldiers and scouts, traveled to colonial capitals as ambassadors, attended colonial colleges as students, walked the streets of colonial towns as visitors, came to settlements as peddlers, and worked as slaves, servants, interpreters, guides, laborers, carpenters, whalers, and sailors. . . .

VIOLENT DISRUPTIONS

For thousands of Indian people, the new world that Europeans created was also a graveyard. European and African people brought with them lethal diseases common in the Old World but unknown in America. Smallpox, plague, measles, influenza, pneumonia, tuberculosis, diphtheria, yellow fever, and a host of new diseases took hold in Indian America and produced one of human history's greatest biological catastrophes. Whole communities perished. Others lost 50 percent, 75 percent, or 90 percent of their population. Recurrent epidemics of the same or different diseases prevented population recovery. European travelers in Indian country saw abandoned villages and met stunned survivors. . . . European invaders confronted Indian people whose capacity to resist often had been seriously eroded before they laid eyes on the enemy. British Indian superintendent Sir William Johnson had the Mohawks inoculated against small-pox, but "contagious Distempers" continued to thin Iroquois numbers. Most Europeans simply accepted the slaughter; but on at least one occasion the British actively promoted it. When two Delawares came into Fort Pitt for talks during Pontiac's War in 1763, "we gave them two Blankets and an Handkerchief out of the Smallpox Hospital," wrote William Trent in his journal. "I hope it will have the desired effect." It did.

The new world that emerged in the wake of European contact was also one of unprecedented violence. Social disruption created random individual violence; warfare reached new levels of in-tensity. Indians fought each other for access to European guns, then turned the guns on their enemies with deadly effect. In-creasingly dependent upon European allies for the goods and guns vital to survival in a dangerous new world, they found it dif-ficult if not impossible to avoid becoming involved in the wars for empire waged in North America. George Morgan, American In-dian agent at Fort Pitt, knew that Indian neutrality in the Revolu-tion was unlikely: "They have long been taught by contending Nations to be bought & sold." Intertribal warfare escalated and, again, Europeans sometimes worked to curtail it, sometimes ac-tively encouraged it as part of a "divide and conquer" strategy. . . .

POVERTY AND DEPENDENCE

Most Indian communities were economically dependent upon Europeans to some degree by 1775. The rate and extent of de-pendency varied, but Cherokees in the mountains of the interior were no more willing or able to do without European trade goods than were coastal groups surrounded by European settlers. A Cherokee headman named Skiagunsta told the governor of South Carolina in 1753 that his people could not survive without the English: "The Cloaths we wear, we cannot make ourselves, they are made to us. We use their Ammunition with which we kill Dear [sic]. We cannot make our Guns, they are made to us. Every necessary Thing in Life we must have from the white People." Skiagunsta probably exaggerated for his audience—In-dian peoples in New England, the Ohio Valley, and the Southeast had learned to overcome total dependence on Europeans by re-pairing and maintaining their own firearms and metal tools—but the language of abject poverty and dependence was common in Indian speeches up through the Revolution. Captain Ouma of the Choctaws said his people were as "helpless as the Beasts in the woods," without British goods; Handsome Fellow of the Oak-fuskie Creeks acknowledged in 1777 that "we have been used so

long to wrap up our Children as soon as they are born in Goods
procured of the white People that we cannot do without it." De-
pendency rendered Indian people vulnerable to abuse: Choctaws
at the Mobile congress in the winter of 1771–2 complained graphically that traders shortchanged them so often that the flaps of
cloth provided as loin cloths "dont cover our secret parts, and we
are in danger of being deprived of our manhood by every hungry dog that approaches."

As Indian peoples became tied into the trade networks of
western Europe, they also became participants in a consumer
revolution that brought the products of industrializing Europe
to frontier America. A "pan-Indian trade culture" emerged in
many areas of the country. . . . By the time of the Revolution, according to one observer, the Fort Hunter Mohawks lived "much
better than most of the Mohawk River farmers." Oneida Indians
cooked in metal kettles and frying pans, ate with spoons from
pewter plates at meals illuminated by candlesticks, sipped out of
teacups filled from teapots, served beverages from punch bowls,
combed their hair with ivory combs while looking in glass mir-
rors, wore white flannel breeches, used silk handkerchiefs, and
lived in "a very large framed house [with a] chimney at each end
[and] painted windows." Overhill Cherokees used combs, mir-
rors, scissors, pewter spoons, and a variety of metal tools and
jewelry. White Eyes of the Delawares and Oconostota of the
Cherokees both wore eyeglasses. . . . Native Americans, like their
backcountry colonial neighbors, had been drawn into a larger Atlantic economy that shaped their tastes, their lives, and ultimately their landscape. For many Indian peoples, the most pressing question posed by the outbreak of the Revolution was not
who should govern in America but who would supply the trade
goods on which they had come to depend. . . .

WHITES LIVING AS INDIANS

Throughout Indian country, Europeans lived in and around Indian communities. Traders who went into Indian country to do
business often found that they were most successful if they married into the kinship networks of Indian societies. Like other
colonists who lived with Indians, many found themselves living
as Indians. Rev. David Jones found 20 whites living at the
Shawnee town of Chillicothe in the winter of 1772–3; as many as
300 English and Scots were living among the Creeks by the beginning of the Revolution. Scotsman Alexander Cameron married a Cherokee woman and lived with the Overhill Cherokees
so long that he "had almost become one of themselves" by the
time of the Revolution.

Many other captives, traders, Indian agents, and even occasional missionaries underwent similar "conversion" to Indian ways. Like many of his Jesuit colleagues, Sebastian Rasles, missionary to the Abenakis at Norridgewock in Maine in the early eighteenth century, spent most of his adult life in Indian country. He spoke the Abenakis' language and shared their homes and hopes, food and fears, even as he sought to convert them. "As for what concerns me personally, Rasles told his brother, "I assure you that I see, that I hear, that I speak, only as a savage."

"White Indians" often aroused fear and contempt in colonial society, but found a place in Indian country and exercised considerable influence as culture brokers. James Dean, who served as an American interpreter during the Revolution, spent his boyhood among the Oneidas and learned to speak their language without a trace of an accent. . . .

Intermarriage between Indians and Europeans, and between Indians and Africans, produced "new peoples" of mixed ancestry. Most were incorporated into Indian communities, but many suffered psychological stress as racial conflicts increased. Some lived with racism in colonial communities; some developed separate communities and formed an ethnic identity of their own. Interaction between different peoples produced new languages in these new worlds. Refugee communities sometimes produced a babel of different dialects. Trade jargons emerged. Indians adopted Spanish, English, Gaelic, Dutch, French, and African words; Europeans incorporated Algonkian, Iroquoian, and Muskhogean terms into their vocabulary. In the 1750s, at Stockbridge, Massachusetts, where an Indian blew a conch shell every Sabbath to call the faithful to worship, the missionary's son heard so much more Mahican than English spoken that he frequently found himself thinking in the Indians' language. Traveling in New York in 1776, Joseph Bloomfield, then a captain in the Third New Jersey Regiment and later governor of New Jersey, heard spoken on a daily basis English, High Dutch, Low Dutch, French, Mohawk, Oneida, Seneca, Cayuga, Onondaga, and Tuscarora.

THE DAUNTING POLITICS OF REVOLUTION

JOHN ROBERTS

The American Revolution was more than a war between two opposing sides. It was a historic alteration in government organization. From the inception of the Continental Congress before the war to the Constitutional Convention after victory was declared, the nation's founders were forced to confront dozens of daunting problems on the road to independence. As author and respected historian John Roberts writes, it was not at all obvious at the time that the grand American experiment would succeed.

D uring the night of 18 April 1775, a detachment of British soldiers marched out of the Massachusetts port of Boston. They were going to the village of Concord, about eighteen miles away, to seize arms and ammunition gathered there by local patriots who feared and sometimes hoped that quarrels then going on with the British government might force Americans to fight to defend their interests. By the morning, when it was light but misty, the British were marching into Lexington, rather more than half-way to their objective. There, something happened which has never been completely explained, for firing began when they encountered a hastily assembled detachment of militia organized by the American patriots. Eight Americans were killed. The British force pushed on to encounter much more formidable opposition later that morning in a long action at Concord bridge before the march back to Boston began.

Excerpted from *Revolution and Improvement: The Western World, 1775–1847,* by John Roberts. Copyright © 1976 John Roberts. Reprinted by permission of the University of California Press.

All the way the British were sniped at and harried, and suffered over two hundred casualties. But what had happened was more important than even this figure suggested, for the War of American Independence had begun.

This was one of those rare moments in world history when great processes and issues run together to be crystallized briefly in a single incident. Later, an American poet wrote of the shots at Concord bridge being heard round the world, and hyperbole for once seems appropriate: this scuffle announced the birth of what was to become the most powerful nation in the world. Few could have seen this coming, but many people had long been expecting to hear the shots. A succession of irritations and grievances had bedevilled relations between the colonies and the mother country for a decade. The most radically minded Americans exploited them until in 1774 things were so bad that Boston, one of the greatest American ports, was occupied by a British garrison and was closed to commerce. A "Continental Congress" met in Philadelphia and formulated proposals to be put to the British government for the pacification of the colonies which went very far. . . .

Soon, radical-minded Americans were able to go much further than this. After the Continental Congress which they dominated there appeared a clearly illegal and revolutionary "Association" to enforce economic sanctions against the British and therefore to supervise much of the daily life of Americans. This was the background of the Concord skirmish. A few weeks later, the British soldiers found themselves bottled up in Boston, besieged by swarms of colonial militiamen dug in on the hills and shores surrounding the city.

THE WAR HAS BEGUN

When, on 10 May, the Continental Congress met, again it was reminded by a delegate from Virginia that "the war is actually begun." Revolt was breaking out everywhere. The law-abiding and moderate who still sought a solution at least under the rule of King George had lost control to the radicals. Congress could only recognize this fact; a "Declaration on the Causes and Necessity of Taking up Arms" was agreed. Still, the final step to independence was not yet taken, though Congress appointed [George Washington as] a commander-in-chief of the forces of the "United Colonies." A British force was bloodily handled at Bunker Hill on 17 June and an American attack was launched on Quebec, the key to former French Canada. But the British government was not disposed to be conciliatory even without such irritations. The radicals continued to fan the flames provided by the propaganda use they could make of American casualties, a process which had begun at once at Lexington, whose eight dead "minutemen" were depicted as helpless victims of unprovoked attack. The British therefore proclaimed the colonies to be in a state of rebellion. General Washington . . . ran up a new flag—of red and white stripes—at his [headquarters] on 1 January 1776. Yet the king's health was still drunk in the officers' mess over which he presided.

In May 1776 Rhode Island was the first colony to declare itself independent. A new Continental Congress at Philadelphia appointed a committee to draft constitutional arrangements for a union of the colonies. There were important divisions about the way ahead. By and large, the radicals wanted the units which were now emerging from the colonial structure to stay as independent as possible; they had on their side the indisputable fact that the states—as we may now call them—of the future nation had come into existence before the Union between them. Conservatives, on the other hand, favoured a stronger central authority. This question was to take years to settle. Meanwhile, the constitutional fate of a new nation would be shaped not only by the ideas and assumptions inherited from the [English] past but . . . the course of hostilities with Great Britain and a public opinion now broadly committed to independence.

On 4 July Congress approved one of the key documents of modern history, the Declaration of Independence, the ideological justification of a new nation. The Virginian [Thomas] Jefferson, who did most of the drafting, claimed that it was "an expression of the American mind," a statement of what was already accepted by American common sense. In part the Declaration was a narrative of the misdeeds of [English king] George III (his parliament's role was all but ignored) [in hostilities against the colonies] as evidence of an attempt to establish a tyranny. This historical case was then used to justify independence, on the basis of a political theory whose essence was the revolutionary claim that governments are set up in order to secure to men their possession of certain rights and that their just powers are derived only from the consent of the governed to this end. For the first time, a major state was to be based wholly on a contractual theory and on popular sovereignty. There would be no place in it for the [dictates of kings] which were so important in the [law] and political theory of every other state in the Western World, and it would be a doctrine which would go the round of the globe.

DIFFICULT AND COSTLY WAR

The war, meanwhile, had to be fought and won if American independence was to survive. Although they suffered a grave and decisive defeat at Saratoga in 1777, the advantage long appeared to lie with the British, who were able to press the Americans hard and had many sympathizers among the colonists (some eighty thousand "loyalists" eventually emigrated to remain under the British flag and many more than this number must have existed in 1776). The colonies' governments did not co-operate easily and were reluctant to pay for defence when not directly menaced, too. Balancing these advantages, on the other hand, was geography—British strategy had to be [expensively] carried out in a huge and widely dispersed group of theatres at the end of more than three thousand miles of oceanic communications. . . . The British had to recover lost dominions; fighting a battle for the hearts and minds of men, they could not terrorize the local population. Destroying the "Continental Army" commanded by General Washington would eliminate the military problem but still leave the political.

Periodically after 1776 each side made gestures towards some settlement which would preserve a formal link between the two largely Anglo-Saxon communities, but the war went on. In the end it was decided by the entry to it of the French in 1778, prompted by the American victory at Saratoga. The Spanish and the Dutch later joined France. Great Britain was the greatest naval power of the age, but this was too great a threat for her fleet to contain while preserving her communications with North America. The end came when a French fleet arrived off the coast of Virginia, where, in October 1781, the British army was bottled up on land by Washington. The siege of Yorktown ended on 17 October, when the British commander surrendered.

Though the war still went on, Yorktown was an event of huge importance. Only seven thousand or so British troops surrendered—about half a modern division—but it was the greatest military disgrace suffered by Great Britain until [the beginning of World War II]. It ended a ministry in London and led George III to draft a message of abdication, though, fortunately, he did not use it. Peace negotiations now began. Hostilities ended at the beginning of 1783, and peace was signed at Paris in the following September.

GIVING POWER TO THE STATES

The new nation had been organizing itself for years. Several states had quickly given themselves constitutions in [a great] burst of political creativity. . . . Two of them were submitted to popular ratification, thus establishing the characteristic American model of distinguishing between constitutional and ordinary legislation, by giving the formulation of the first to a special [Constitutional] Convention and then having it approved by some kind of referendum. . . . Though republican in form, they retained governors who exercised the executive power and two legislative chambers. Usually, the electorate was limited.

At the national level it had soon been obvious, above all in foreign affairs and commerce, that Congress had to exercise some central authority. Articles of Confederation were drawn up, but they were not accepted by all states and effective until 1781. These Articles clearly left the [power with] the individual states; a Congress of Confederation was set up with the same powers already enjoyed by the Continental Congress. But new issues had increased tension between those who favoured more centralization and those who favoured the rights of the states. In particular, they arose over the future use and relation to the new nation of Western lands, and over the weight to be given . . . to slaves in computing the representation to be given to states. The Articles of Confederation had just sustained the government in war but proved barely adequate even for that. It was more true that the British had lost the war than that the Americans had won it.

Post-war difficulties seemed to show that the Continental Congress could neither tax the states nor control their monetary policies in a time of economic difficulty and thus restore public credit, nor provide force to uphold the law when a state asked for it. For many Americans the crucial evidence that a new Constitution was needed came in 1786 when a rebellion of Massachusetts farmers [fomented a violent revolt known as Shays's Rebellion and] Congress was powerless to help. It seemed that the break up into anarchy [of the new country] which was the fate often predicted for the new republic [by critics] was now about to take place. It was time for a change.

THE SUCCESSFUL CONSTITUTION

A Constitutional Convention met at Philadelphia in May 1787. Debate was long and difficult. It was also, so far as incomplete records reveal, of a remarkably high standard. The central issue was the power to be given to the national government. From the start, those who sought a strong national focus took the initiative but they had to relinquish many of their hopes. On the other hand, the federal government which emerged from the deliberations of the Founding Fathers reflected their wishes more than those of their opponents. A league of states was transformed into a nation, the device of delimiting the areas of action of the national government and that of the states being the key to this solution. The smaller states which had feared that the larger states would have too much weight in a stronger union were reassured by concessions made to them. The whole structure was negoti-

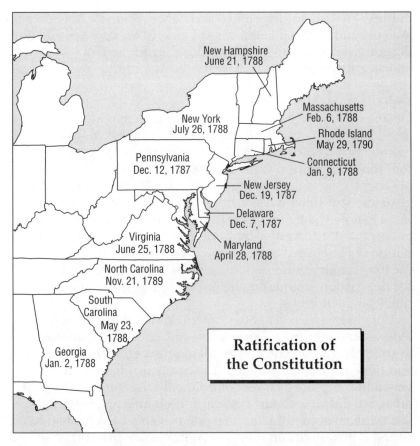

New Hampshire
June 21, 1788

Massachusetts
Feb. 6, 1788

New York
July 26, 1788

Rhode Island
May 29, 1790

Pennsylvania
Dec. 12, 1787

Connecticut
Jan. 9, 1788

New Jersey
Dec. 19, 1787

Delaware
Dec. 7, 1787

Virginia
June 25, 1788

Maryland
April 28, 1788

North Carolina
Nov. 21, 1789

South
Carolina
May 23,
1788

**Ratification of
the Constitution**

Georgia
Jan. 2, 1788

ated, realistic, a compromise. Though one state was to hold out until 1790, a sufficient majority had ratified the Constitution for the first presidency of the United States, that of George Washington, to be inaugurated on 30 April 1789.

The Constitution was to prove astonishingly successful. Through interpretation and amendment, it was able to regulate the transformation of the United States from an agrarian to an industrial society and from a scatter of weak and isolated little republics to a nation of global power. The success it enjoyed can be measured by its durability. . . . Gradually, its example and influence would be felt worldwide, though this would take a long time. The device of a written constitution, as opposed to the charter of liberties or privileges, was an American invention. . . . Because of this its fundamentals were especially important, above all the principle of popular sovereignty. Yet the Founding Fathers deployed it not to draw up a scheme of government for Utopia but to meet pressing needs, as the opening words of the Constitution show: "We the People of the United States, in order to form a more perfect union, establish Justice, insure domestic tran-

quillity, provide for the common defence, promote the general
Welfare, and secure the Blessings of Liberty to ourselves and our
Posterity, do ordain and establish this Constitution for the United
States of America."

A GREAT EXPERIMENT

Of course, more was at stake in principle than whether treaties
could be honoured or debts collected. It is now taken so much for
granted that it is easy to overlook the supremely important point
that the Constitution was republican. This implied a great experiment. One of the leading members of the Convention said a
great and true thing when he reminded his colleagues at one moment that they were to decide the fate of republican [democratic]
government. Its prestige in modern times dates from the foundation of the United States. It was perhaps the turning-point in
the long history of the republican idea when it was settled that
the new nation, unique among great powers, would maintain republican institutions. . . .

Thus in fourteen years the American Revolution had come a
long way. Yet the events that followed Concord also constituted
a strangely limited change, for all their expense and bloodshed
and huge future implications. The essence of the revolution . . .
was that it replaced one set of political arrangements with another, but did so without . . . social or economic upheaval, though
such upheaval might later be made possible by what had happened. The revolution was also conservative in another sense.
Whatever individual Americans might think then and later about
their country's duty to uphold abroad the principles on which it
rested, the American revolution was unaggressive and for a long
time bred few missionaries. Geography helped; the new union
was a far-off country with little interest in what went on in Europe. The achievement of the American revolution opened the
way to nationhood for Americans. Its exemplification of certain
political principles was to be very important in the long run in
shaping ideals elsewhere, but the direct importance of the American Revolution was that it made a nation and changed the history of a hemisphere.

THOMAS PAINE'S COMMON SENSE

THOMAS PAINE

When Thomas Paine published the political pamphlet *Common Sense* in January 1776, it sold over one hundred thousand copies in three months and inspired many American revolutionaries to take up arms against the British monarchy. Although his words have represented the basic American philosophies toward government for centuries, Paine was actually an English excise tax officer who did not move to the colonies until 1774. In the following excerpt Paine paints a negative picture of Britain's interference with American society and justifies the violence of the American Revolution.

Society in every state is a blessing, but government, even in its best state, is but a necessary evil; in its worst state an intolerable one: for when we suffer, or are exposed to the same miseries *by a government*, which we might expect in a country *without government*, our calamity is heightened by reflecting that we furnish the means by which we suffer. Government, like dress, is the badge of lost innocence; the palaces of kings are built upon the ruins of the bowers of paradise. For were the impulses of conscience clear, uniform and irresistibly obeyed, man would need no other law-giver; but that not being the case, he finds it necessary to surrender up a part of his property to furnish means for the protection of the rest; and this he is induced to do by the same prudence which in every other case advises him, out of two evils to choose the least. Wherefore, security being the true design and end of government, it unanswerably follows that what-

From "Common Sense," by Thomas Paine, 1776. (This version taken from *Selected Writings of Thomas Paine*, edited by Richard Emery. New York: Everybody's Vacation Publishing Co., 1945.)

ever form thereof appears most likely to ensure it to us, with the least expense and greatest benefit, is preferable to all others.

In order to gain a clear and just idea of the design and end of government, let us suppose a small number of persons settled in some sequestered part of the earth, unconnected with the rest; they will then represent the first peopling of any country, or of the world. In this state of natural liberty, society will be their first thought. A thousand motives will excite them thereto; the strength of one man is so unequal to his wants, and his mind so unfitted for perpetual solitude, that he is soon obliged to seek assistance and relief of another, who in his turn requires the same. Four or five united would be able to raise a tolerable dwelling in the midst of a wilderness, but one man might labor out the common period of life without accomplishing any thing; when he had felled his timber he could not remove it, nor erect it after it was removed; hunger in the mean time would urge him to quit his work, and every different want would call him a different way. Disease, nay even misfortune, would be death; for though neither might be mortal, yet either would disable him from living, and reduce him to a state in which he might rather be said to perish than to die.

Thus necessity . . . would soon form our newly arrived emigrants into society, the reciprocal blessings of which would supercede, and render the obligations of law and government unnecessary while they remained perfectly just to each other; but as nothing but Heaven is impregnable to vice, it will unavoidably happen that in proportion as they surmount the first difficulties of emigration, which bound them together in a common cause, they will begin to relax in their duty and attachment to each other: and this remissness will point out the necessity of establishing some form of government to supply the defect of moral virtue.

THE VOICE OF REASON

Some convenient tree will afford them a State House, under the branches of which the whole colony may assemble to deliberate on public matters. It is more than probable that their first laws will have the title only of regulations and be enforced by no other penalty than public disesteem. In this first parliament every man by natural right will have a seat.

But as the colony increases, the public concerns will increase likewise, and the distance at which the members may be separated, will render it too inconvenient for all of them to meet on every occasion as at first, when their number was small, their habitations near, and the public concerns few and trifling. This will point out the convenience of their consenting to leave the legislative part to be managed by a select number chosen from the whole body, who are supposed to have the same concerns at stake which those who have appointed them, and who will act in the same manner as the whole body would act were they present. If the colony continue increasing, it will become necessary to augment the number of representatives, and that the interest of every part of the colony may be attended to, it will be found best to divide the whole into convenient parts, each part sending its proper

Thomas Paine

number: and that the *elected* might never form to themselves an interest separate from the *electors,* prudence will point out the propriety of having elections often: because as the *elected* might by that means return and mix again with the general body of the *electors* in a few months, their fidelity to the public will be secured by the prudent reflection of not making a rod for themselves. And as this frequent interchange will establish a common interest with every part of the community, they will mutually and naturally support each other, and on this . . . depends the *strength of government, and the happiness of the governed.*

Here then is the origin and rise of government; namely, a mode rendered necessary by the inability of moral virtue to govern the world; here too is the design and end of government, viz. freedom and security. And however our eyes may be dazzled with show, or our ears deceived by sound; however prejudice may warp our wills, or interest darken our understanding, the simple voice of nature and reason will say, 'tis right. . . .

COMMON SENSE

In the following pages I offer nothing more than simple facts, plain arguments, and common sense. . . .

Volumes have been written on the subject of the struggle between England and America. Men of all ranks have embarked in the controversy, from different motives, and with various designs; but all have been ineffectual, and the period of debate is closed. Arms as the last resource decide the contest; the appeal was the choice of the king, and the continent has accepted the challenge. . . .

The sun never shone on a cause of greater worth. 'Tis not the affair of a city, a county, a province, or a kingdom; but of a continent—of at least one eighth part of the habitable globe. 'Tis not the concern of a day, a year, or an age; posterity are virtually involved in the contest, and will be more or less affected even to the end of time, by the proceedings now. Now is the seed-time of continental union, faith and honor. The least fracture now will be like a name engraved with the point of a pin on the tender rind of a young oak; the wound would enlarge with the tree, and posterity read it in full grown characters.

By referring the matter from argument to arms, a new æra for politics is struck—a new method of thinkings has arisen. All plans, proposals, &c. prior to the nineteenth of April [1775], *i.e.* to the commencement of hostilities, are like the almanacks of the last year; which though proper then, are superceded and useless now. . . .

As much has been said of the advantages of reconciliation, which, like an agreeable dream, has passed away and left us as we were, it is but right that we should examine the contrary side of the argument, and inquire into some of the many material injuries which these colonies sustain, and always will sustain, by being connected with and dependant on Great Britain. To examine that connection and dependance, on the principles of nature and common sense, to see what we have to trust to, if separated, and what we are to expect, if dependant.

I have heard it asserted by some, that as America has flourished under her former connection with Great Britain, the same connection is necessary towards her future happiness, and will always have the same effect. Nothing can be more fallacious than this kind of argument. We may as well assert that because a child has thrived upon milk, that it is never to have meat, or that the first twenty years of our lives is to become a precedent for the next twenty. But even this is admitting more than is true; for I answer roundly, that America would have flourished as much, and probably much more, had no European power taken any notice of her. The commerce by which she hath enriched herself are the necessaries of life, and will always have a market while eating is the custom of Europe.

THE PHILOSOPHY BEHIND THE IDEAS OF THE AMERICAN REVOLUTION

CLINTON ROSSITER

The widespread popularity of the American Revolution among average citizens was the result of dozens of pamphlets, books, and articles that expounded on weighty topics such as the inalienable rights of man and the individual's natural place in society. Revolutionary philosophers believed that every white male, no matter what his station in life, was capable of understanding and participating in enlightened self-government.

By educating the common person to the virtues of liberty and democracy, leaders of the Revolutionary War were able to rally the majority of the American people to their cause.

In the 1960s Clinton Rossiter was the professor of American institutions at Cornell University and a professor of American history at Cambridge University.

T he American consensus dictated no particular estimate of the nature of man. Patriot philosophers with identical opinions about the [powers] of sovereignty could entertain the most divergent views about the reasoning powers of men, and a single thinker might advance two or three different estimates within the pages of one tract. A good deal depended, of course, upon the author's immediate purpose. An argument for

Excerpted from "American Political Thought, 1765–1776," in *Seedtime of the Republic: The Origin of the American Tradition of Political Liberty*, by Clinton Rossiter. Copyright © 1953 Clinton Rossiter, renewed 1981 by Mary Crane Rossiter, Caleb Rossiter, David Rossiter, and Winston Rossiter. Reprinted by permission of Harcourt, Inc.

[American] rule would lead him to sweeping generalizations about self-reliance and sociability. A tirade against the British ministry would evoke equally broad comments about man's vicious nature. We must remember that the colonists were heirs of several great and cross-cutting traditions. A son of the Puritans who was also a child of the Enlightenment could be indulged a little confusion on this crucial point.

A Slave to Passions

We may reduce the wide range of opinion on the nature of man to three general attitudes. One small group of thinkers, of whom [Thomas] Jefferson was perhaps the boldest, took the "enlightened" view, considering man a naturally good, decent, friendly, capable person whose troubles were the bitter fruit of a world he had never made. Another, to which many Calvinist preachers belonged, clung to doctrines of sin and depravity, preferring to lay stress, as did [clergyman] John Witherspoon, on "the ignorance, prejudice, partiality and injustice of human nature." Most thinkers settled down between these two extremes, finding much that was good and much that was bad in the character of every single man. Said the [unnamed] author of a piece entitled "Loose thoughts on GOVERNMENT" in the *Virginia Gazette* in 1776:

> In whatever situation we take a view of man, whether ranging the forests in the rude state of his primeval existence, or in the smooth situation of polished society; wheresoever we place him, on the burning sands of Africa, the freezing coasts of Labrador, or the more congenial climes of the temperate zones, we shall every where find him the same complex being, a slave to his passions, and tossed and agitated by a thousand disagreeing virtues and discordant vices.

Four Good Qualities

What exactly were those fundamental traits that Revolutionary thinkers found ingrained in man? Which ones were most significant for political organization?

Four qualities that our culture considers "good" were given special stress in the literature of the Revolution: *sociability*, the impulse to associate and co-operate with other men in pursuit of common ends; *love of liberty*, which makes it unnatural and therefore impossible for a man to submit to slavery; *goodness*, the quality of basic human decency that inspires every man, in the words of John Adams, to "a love of truth, and a veneration for virtue"; and *rationality*, the ability to read, understand, and apply "the

eternal laws of natural justice, humanity and equity." Five qualities that we would consider "bad" were stressed with equal
vigor, as often as not by the same authors who extolled man's
goodness: *selfishness*, the impulse to seek one's own happiness
even in defiance of the common good; *depravity*, the quality of
sinfulness—of jealousy, injustice, anger, ignorance, deceit, van-
ity, and intemperance—that lurks in every human soul; *passion*,
the refusal to be rational, which Rev. Phillips Payson found to be
"as natural to men as reason" itself; *moral laziness*, "Inattention to
the real Importance of things," which brings men to slavery contrary to nature and their wills; and *corruptibility*, the inevitable result of "the passion for acquiring power" which operates so
"forcibly on the human mind." All these "disagreeing virtues and
discordant vices" were thought to be present to some degree in
every man, no matter how lofty his station or low his character.

Perhaps the most politically significant of all these qualities
was sociability, the urge man feels to associate with other men,
even if this means surrendering a substantial part of his original
freedom. So pointed was the emphasis placed upon "the social
Principle in man" that many thinkers excluded the pre-social
state of nature, and therefore natural man, from serious consideration. Man was clearly a social animal, [Revolutionary War
hero] Joseph Warren observed, a being "formed for social life."
If he had a natural state, that state was society, [colonial leader]
James Otis agreed, for "'tis clear that men cannot live apart or independent of each other." Society itself was therefore natural,
and few men if any could be said to be in it by free choice. While
American thinkers were understandably confused in this matter,
it seems clear that the most thoughtful of them made a distinction between society and government. The former was the "natural" result of the presence of a number of men in a certain area;
the latter was the mechanistic if inevitable result of an act of will.
In short, the contract in Revolutionary thought was governmental, not social.

THE SEEDS OF TYRANNY

The one other quality deserving special mention was the transformation that is more than likely to come over man when he is
placed in a situation of power. Revolutionary thinkers, beset by
threats of arbitrary British policy, generally agreed with [Alexan-
der] Hamilton that "a fondness for power is implanted in most
men, and it is natural to abuse it when acquired." "The history
of mankind," [jurist] James Iredell wrote, "unhappily justifies the
strongest suspicion of men in authority." "Every man by nature,"
Rev. Thomas Allen of Pittsfield echoed, "has the seeds of tyranny

deeply implanted within him." Although this belief in man's love of power was not nearly so strong or widely advertised as it was later to be in Federalist political thought, few authors failed to mention it as a human characteristic, and none went out of his way to deny it specifically. The universal American belief in constitutionalism and the rule of law—indeed in the necessity of a written, comprehensible constitution—derived from this suspicious appraisal of man in authority. No one ever spoke more succinctly to this point than [Revolutionary leader] Samuel Adams:

> All men are fond of Power. It is difficult for us to be prevaild upon to believe that we possess more than belongs to us. Even publick Bodies of men legally constituted are too prone to covet more Power than the Publick hath judgd it safe to entrust them with. It is happy when their Power is not only subject to Controul while it is exercisd, but frequently reverts into the hands of the People from whom it is derived, and to whom Men in Power ought for ever to be accountable.

If man was a composite of good and evil, of ennobling excellencies and degrading imperfections, then one of the chief ends of the community, an anonymous Virginian advised, was "to separate his virtues from his vices," to help him purposefully to pursue his better nature. The achievement of this purpose called for two types of collective action: establishing or encouraging institutions, especially religious and political institutions, that would give free play to his virtues while controlling or suppressing his vices; educating him to recognize the sweet harvest of the one and bitter fruits of the other. True religion encouraged man to suppress his savage impulses; constitutional government forced him to think before acting; sound education taught him the delights of virtue and liberty.

A Capacity for Learning

Whatever disagreement might have existed over man's other natural or social characteristics, all American thinkers conceded him a capacity for learning. Different men could acquire knowledge in different amounts, but all men could acquire the minimum necessary for survival and citizenship. Man was something more than a fortuitous complex of virtues and vices. He was *educable*—he could learn and be taught. More to the point, he could learn why to cherish virtue and shun vice, how to serve the community and defend liberty. Free government rested on virtue, virtue on knowledge, knowledge on regular techniques of education. It was therefore the business of government, Rev. Simeon Howard pointed out in 1780, "to make provision for schools and all suitable means of instruction." The exigencies of the economy, the weight of tradition, and the unsettled state of the times conspired against general acceptance of the doctrine of free and universal public education, yet no political thinker doubted the imperative necessity of community action in this crucial area. The eloquent words of Rev. Phillips Payson expressed American thinking about education for liberty in the darkest year of the struggle, 1778:

> The slavery of a people is generally founded in ignorance of some kind or another; and there are not wanting such facts as abundantly prove the human mind may be so sunk and debased, through ignorance and its natural effects, as even to adore its enslaver, and kiss its chains. Hence knowledge and learning may well be considered as most essentially requisite to a free, righteous government. . . .

> Every kind of useful knowledge will be carefully encouraged and promoted by the rulers of a free state. . . . The education of youth, by instructors properly qualified, the establishment of societies for useful arts and sciences, the encouragement of persons of superior abilities, will always command the attention of wise rulers.

Political thinkers naturally emphasized the acquisition of political knowledge. Said [future Supreme Court justice] John Jay on the inauguration of the New York Constitution of 1777:

> Let virtue, honor, the love of liberty and of science be, and remain, the soul of this constitution, and it will become the source of great and extensive happiness to this and future generations. Vice, ignorance, and want of vigilance, will be the only enemies able to destroy it. Against these provide, and, of these, be forever jealous. Every member of the state, ought diligently to read and study the constitution of his country, and teach the rising generation to be free. By knowing their rights, they will sooner perceive when they are violated, and be the better prepared to defend and assert them.

Others called attention to the mutual dependence of liberty and learning. Education and knowledge were as much the effect as the cause of free government. The infant republic could look forward confidently to intellectual splendor. Dr. David Ramsay [a Continental Congress delegate] was one of many who prophesied:

> Every circumstance concurs to make it probable, that the arts and sciences will be cultivated, extended, and

improved, in independent America. . . . Our free governments are the proper nurseries of rhetoric, criticism,
and the arts which are founded on the philosophy of
the human mind. . . . It is hoped, that the free governments of America will produce poets, orators, critics
and historians, equal to the most celebrated of the ancient commonwealths of Greece and Italy.

While many Americans may have smiled at the grandeur of
this hope, few doubted the capacity of "this numerous, brave and
hardy people" to learn the rights and duties of citizenship in a free
republic. No characteristic of man had more political significance
than his innate capacity for instruction in virtue and freedom. . . .

THE RIGHT TO LIBERTY

The natural right to liberty was central to all other rights, and the
literature of the Revolution is full of salutes to its blessings and
excellencies. "Liberty!" had been the American watchword for
so many generations that no author . . . ever doubted in print that
it was, as James Iredell wrote, "in some degree . . . the right of
every human creature." Indeed, man without natural liberty was
a contradiction in terms. "The god who gave us life," Jefferson
wrote to George III, "gave us liberty at the same time." Liberty
was defined simply as the freedom and power of each individual to act as he pleased "without restraint or control." From this
natural liberty, the freedom from "obligation to obedience,"
flowed all other liberties that men enjoyed in society.

Americans, of course, were concerned about specific liberties
in the political community rather than the original liberty of man
in the state of nature. Most of their discussions of liberty are
therefore somewhat confused. . . . A good example of the way in
which the colonial thinker dealt with liberty is a communication
of 1765 to the *New-York Gazette*:

Liberty, as it is the honour and glory of a nation, so also
it is their pleasure and happiness. There is not perhaps
one temporal blessing bestowed by the supreme being
on mankind that is more agreeable when enjoyed; more
difficult to be parted with; or more desirable when ab-
sent. A love for Liberty seems interwoven with our very
nature; and we are always ready to pronounce a people
happy or miserable in proportion as they are possessed
or destitute of it. . . . There is perhaps nothing in this life
more essential to our happiness. It is the state for which
we are naturally calculated. It is what we all desire. The
absence of it produces positive pain, as well as the pres-

ence of it positive happiness. It is the fountain of
wealth, and of all real honours. For I cannot conceive of
any true dignity a Slave can enjoy; for although he com-
mands a thousand or ten thousand others, he is yet but
a Slave himself.

Colonial thinkers, even the holders of slaves, concurred generally with this author's assumption that all men were naturally
free. Most arguments for abolition of Negro slavery advanced in
the Revolution were based on the doctrine of natural, unalien-
able liberty.

Perhaps the most interesting subsidiary right that Revolutionary pamphleteers deduced from natural liberty was, in the
words of Jefferson,

a right, which nature has given to all men, of depart-
ing from the country in which chance, not choice has
placed them, of going in quest of new habitations, and
of there establishing new societies, under such laws
and regulations as to them shall seem most likely to
promote public happiness.

BLACK SLAVES DECLARE THEIR INDEPENDENCE

BENJAMIN QUARLES

The powerful theories of equal rights and personal freedom used to justify the American Revolution inspired African American slaves—especially those living in the northern colonies—to demand their freedom as well. The simple phrase *All men are created equal* from the Declaration of Independence was quoted again and again by blacks who petitioned state legislatures and governors to outlaw slavery and grant blacks equal status with whites. Because of the large number of protests and lawsuits by blacks who took the Declaration of Independence to heart, slavery was voluntarily outlawed by most northern state constitutions nearly eighty years before it was forcibly abolished in the southern states.

African American author Benjamin Quarles is a leading authority on the contributions of blacks to American history. He was born in Boston, was dean of Dillard University in New Orleans until 1953, and head of the department of history at Morgan State College in Baltimore until 1974.

With the outbreak of the Revolutionary War the movement to better the lot of the Negro was accelerated. More weight was given to the contention that slavery was dangerous to the public peace and safety; it was feared that slaves would be more minded to revolt than ever. Also, particularly above the Potomac [River, in the northern colonies], the eco-

Excerpted from *The Negro in the American Revolution*, by Benjamin Quarles. Published for the Omohundro Institute of Early American History and Culture. Copyright © 1997 by the University of North Carolina Press. Used by permission of the publisher.

nomic and utilitarian argument against slavery—that it was not profitable—was more strongly voiced. Finally, the ideals of the Revolution had an effect; the theories set forth to justify economic and political freedom from England could scarcely leave domestic institutions untouched. A master–slave society was repugnant to the revolutionary spirit and to the beliefs in the human freedoms which were its heart.

This spirit of liberty, of so much significance to the unfree, was nowhere better expressed than in the Declaration of Independence. As originally presented to Congress by . . . Thomas Jefferson, the document included a sharp condemnation of the slave trade. [English king] George III, ran the indictment, "has waged cruel war against human nature itself, violating its most sacred rights of life and liberty in the persons of a distant people who never offended him, captivating and carrying them into slavery in another hemisphere, or to incur miserable death in their transportation thither." This clause was stricken from the final draft since it gave offense to some of the Southern delegates (and a few from the North). . . . The growing humanitarian sentiment against slavery therefore found no direct expression in the Declaration of Independence; indeed, the only reference to slavery was the indirectly stated charge that George III had fomented domestic insurrection in America. In *Common Sense* [political writer Thomas] Paine had bluntly accused England of stirring up the Negroes "to destroy us," but in the Declaration, Jefferson dared not be specific and spell out the domestic insurrection charge. To have done so would have called attention to American slavery—an embarrassing topic in a document whose keynote was human freedom.

Despite its omissions and evasions, however, the Declaration of Independence held a great appeal for those who considered themselves oppressed. "All men are created equal," ran the magic words. Perhaps the congressmen who adopted the document intended that the word "equal" was to be narrow and qualified in interpretation. Perhaps the words were not meant to apply to slaves, since men in bondage were not considered constituent members of society. Perhaps the great phrases which assert that among the rights every man is born with are life, liberty, and the pursuit of happiness were intended to be an expression of ideals rather than a plan of social action. Yet the Declaration of Independence would remain a battle cry for freedom. "It did, indeed, at last become very hard for us to listen each year to the preamble to the Declaration of Independence and still remain the owners and users and catchers of slaves," wrote [historian] Moses Coit Tyler. And if Jefferson himself did not fully sense this when he drafted the document, he would come to a

fuller realization some years later when Benjamin Banneker, a
Negro mathematician and astronomer, would write him a long
letter asking him to reconcile his "created equal" language with
his practice of "detaining by fraud and violence so numerous a
part of my brethren, under groaning captivity."

REQUESTING FREEDOM FROM BONDAGE

The Negro was not slow in responding to the revolutionary spirit
of the opening passages of the Declaration of Independence.
New hope came to slaves as the words "liberty" and "independence" became common currency. Giving a personal interpretation to the high-sounding slogans which justified the break with
England, they redoubled their efforts for emancipation.

New England's slaves particularly took heart. Unlike the
mildly worded supplications of pre-war days, their petitions now
took on a note of impatience. In a petition dated January 13, 1777,
a group of Massachusetts Negroes stated that they had long
awaited a favorable response to entreaty after entreaty. Every
principle which impelled America to break with England, they
said, "pleads stronger than a thousand arguments in favor of
your humble petitioners." A life of slavery was "far worse than
Nonexistence." Late in 1779 a group of nineteen Negroes in
Portsmouth, New Hampshire, urged the state to pass a law
whereby they might regain their liberty "and that the name of
slave may not more be heard in a land gloriously contending for
the sweets of freedom." The petitioners pointed out that they
were not complaining of any mistreatment from their masters,
but "we would wish to know . . . from what authority they assume to dispose of our lives, freedom and property."

In the spring of 1779 a group of Connecticut slaves petitioned
the state legislature for their liberty, condemning slavery in the
same breath. They not only "groaned" under their own burdens,
ran their plea, but they contemplated with horror "the miserable
Condition of Our Children, who are training up, and kept in
Preparation, for a like State of Bondage and Servitude." In Connecticut a few petitions came from Negroes whose masters had
fled to the British. In October 1779 [a slave named] Pomp, belonging to a Norwalk Tory, sent a request to the legislature pray-
ing to be set free. A month later eight slaves of William Browne
of Salem, Connecticut, "Great Prince, Little Prince, Luke, Cesar,
and Prue and her three children,—all friends to America," asked
the General Assembly for their freedom. "We hope," they stated,
"that our good mistress, the free State of Connecticut, engaged
in a war with tyranny, will not sell good honest . . . friends of
freedom and independence, as we are." An individual request

was sent in by [a slave named] Belinda who alleged that, although she had been serving her master for more than forty years, her labors had not brought her any comfort or security. She begged freedom for herself and her "poor daughter."

CONDEMNING TYRANNY

Three of the best-known Negroes in Revolutionary America—Prince Hall, Paul Cuffe, and Phillis Wheatley, all of Massachusetts—took a personal role in the agitation. Born in Barbados, Hall had come to America in 1765 and by industry and private study had become fairly well-to-do by the time of the war. Free himself, he made it a point to sign slave petitions for emancipation. . . .

Paul Cuffe was a captain of ships constructed in his own yards. In February 1780 Cuffe, barely twenty-one years old, got up a petition, signed by six others, which was offered to the Massachusetts legislature. It asked that Negroes be relieved from paying taxes, since they had "no voice or influence in the election of those who tax us." A year later Cuffe and his brother requested the selectmen of Dartmouth to give free Negroes and mulattoes the same voting privileges enjoyed by the whites of the town.

Sharing the general hopes of all who had known oppression was the most conspicuous Negro of her brief day, Phillis Wheatley, who had been brought to America while still a little girl. Given every opportunity by the Wheatley family in Boston, she published her first poem in 1770, which was followed three years later by a book of verse, *Poems on Various Subjects, Religious and Moral*. By 1774, although not more than twenty years old, she enjoyed an international reputation; Voltaire knew of her, and referred to her "very good English verse." Her stanzas, patterned after [poet Alexander] Pope, were "echoes of the English classicists," but they were not without their racial and personal elements. In a composition dedicated to the Earl of Dartmouth, whom she had met in London, young Phillis praises liberty, condemns tyranny, then proceeds to account for her own sentiments:

> Should you, my lord, while you peruse my song,
> Wonder from whence my love of Freedom sprung,
>
> I, young in life, by seeming cruel fate
> Was snatch'd from Afric's fancy'd seat:
>
> Such, such my case. And can I then but pray
> Others may never feel tryannic sway?

An occasional poet, Phillis composed a tribute to [George] Washington upon his appointment as commander-in-chief of the army. In the letter which accompanied the poem, Phillis expressed the hope that "your Excellency" would meet with all possible success "in the great cause you are so generously engaged in." Her lines reach the level of panegyric:

> Thee, first in place and honours,—we demand
> The grace and glory of thy martial band.
> Fam'd for thy valour, for thy virtues more,
> Here every tongue thy guardian aid implore!

Washington took some months to acknowledge these lines. On February 10, 1776, he sent the poem to Joseph Reed, adding that the latter might find it amusing. His first impulse, Washington said, was to publish it, but thinking he might be considered vain, he had "laid it aside." Nearly three weeks later Washington wrote to his eulogist, thanking her and adding that he would have had the verse published as a "striking proof of your great poetical talents," but had not done so lest his motives be misconstrued. He would be happy to see her, ran his concluding sentence, if she should ever come to Cambridge or near his headquarters.

ALL ARE BORN FREE AND EQUAL

The pen of a Wheatley, the protest of a Cuffe, and the petition of a Belinda were not without influence above the Potomac. As the war dragged on, the advocates of freedom for the slave found a more receptive public. Among the New England states, Massachusetts was the readiest to let slavery die.

In June 1777, in response to a Negro petition, the Massachusetts legislature drafted a bill for "preventing the practice of holding persons in Slavery." A committee was appointed to prepare a letter to the Continental Congress asking whether such an enactment by Massachusetts might imperil the friendly relations among the states. However, the committee's report, made on the following day, was "ordered to lie."

Slavery in Massachusetts, however, had but a short lease on life. It was dealt a blow by an interpretation which the state courts gave to its constitution. The Massachusetts constitution of 1780, borrowing from the Virginia Bill of Rights and the Declaration of Independence, stipulated that "all men are born free and equal." This phrase seemed to be given a literal interpretation in the celebrated Quok Walker case.

In April 1781 twenty-eight-year-old Walker had run away from his master, Nathaniel Jennison, a Worcester County farmer. The latter brought suit against John Caldwell, a neighbor, who had given Walker asylum and employment. Stating his damages at £1,000, Jennison charged Caldwell with enticing Walker away. In turn, Walker brought suit against Jennison for assault and battery; Jennison, having discovered Walker's whereabouts ten days after his flight, had gone there and beaten him with the handle of a whip.

As revealed by the brief prepared by Levi Lincoln, later United States attorney-general under President Jefferson, the lawyers for Walker and Caldwell based their main plea on the general principles of freedom. Two lines from Lincoln's brief illustrate this approach:

> Mr. Stearns says the custom and usage of the country consider slavery as right.

> Objt. Custom and usages against reason and right, Void.

The master, Jennison, lost his suit against Caldwell, and he lost the suit brought against him by Quok Walker. In the verdicts the Supreme Judicial Court seemed to concur in the opinion that the "born free" clause of the state constitution was to be regarded as an authoritative expression of the law rather than as a high-sounding but legally meaningless rhetorical flourish. By 1783, when the judiciary passed down its final decision in the Jennison case, slavery in Massachusetts was in its death throes.

ABOLISHING SLAVERY IN THE NORTH

No other New England state took such forthright antislavery action during the war. In New Hampshire the assembly twice debated the freedom petition sent in by slaves but on June 9, 1780, postponed the matter "to a more convenient opportunity." In Connecticut the legislature in 1779 set at liberty a Negro slave, Pomp who had petitioned for his freedom, his master having "absconded to the enemy." In the same year, however, the petition of eight slaves of another Tory master was granted by one house of the legislature but not the other. The following year a gradual emancipation bill passed the upper chamber but got no further. In August 1775 the Quaker merchant, Moses Brown, led the movement to prod the Rhode Island legislature into acting on an emancipation measure, but his recommendation did not bear fruit until nine years later. The only Rhode Island legislation against slavery during the war, apart from the partial abolition of the slave trade described earlier, was an act which prohibited selling a slave out of the state without his consent.

The middle states had their anti-slavery advocates. In New Jersey Governor William Livingston asked the assembly in 1778 to pass a manumission law [freeing slaves], stating that slavery was "utterly inconsistent with the principles of Christianity and humanity; and in Americans who have almost idolized liberty, peculiarly odious and disgraceful." In New York Gouverneur Morris, against slavery but fearing immediate emancipation, sought in 1777 to persuade his colleagues in the legislature to instruct the framers of the state constitution to insert into that document a pledge of future liberation. But his colleagues, even more apprehensive than Morris, labeled the proposal "inexpedient," and would give it no further consideration.

To Pennsylvania, with its Quaker background, went the distinction of becoming the first state to abolish slavery. In November 1778 the Council requested the lower chamber to prepare a bill for manumitting infant Negroes born of slaves, but a matter of protocol between the two houses prevented the passing of an act until March 1, 1780. This historic measure was designed to "extend a portion of that freedom to others which has been extended to us." This act did not provide for immediate and outright emancipation; its approach was gradualist. It freed nobody who was then a slave. Henceforth, however, when children of slaves reached twenty-eight years old, they would become free.

The revolutionary spirit of freedom had a marked influence upon America. Just prior to the war this spirit, fanned by humanitarians like Anthony Benezet, found expression in slave petitions for freedom. But sympathy for the Negro was enlivened by the moving prose of the Declaration of Independence, and the wartime fruits of that enlivened sentiment were the curtailment of the slave trade and a movement toward slave manumission, particularly above the Mason-Dixon line. Emancipation measures did not go unopposed, and even when adopted, as in Pennsylvania, their opponents were adept in finding loopholes in the law.

THE ECONOMIC THEORIES OF ADAM SMITH

ADAM SMITH

Scottish native Adam Smith has been called "the Father of Modern Economics." His 1776 book *An Inquiry into the Nature and Causes of the Wealth of Nations* remains one of the most influential treatises on the subject. In the book Smith puts forward the theory that when people are free to pursue their own economic interests—no matter how selfish—society as a whole benefits. Conversely, when governments attempt to regulate market forces, progress is thwarted.

In the following excerpt Smith discusses the power wealthy landlords held over impoverished farmers and laborers, who were forced to pay high rents to work the land. Although Smith's theories were widely accepted in the American colonies, they were inadvertently used to justify revolution against wealthy landlords by poor European peasants in later years.

A s soon as land becomes private property, the landlord demands a share of almost all the produce which the labourer can either raise, or collect from it. His rent makes the first deduction from the produce of the labour which is employed upon land.

It seldom happens that the person who tills the ground has wherewithal to maintain himself till he reaps the harvest. His maintenance is generally advanced to him from the stock of a master, the farmer who employs him, and who would have no

Excerpted from *An Inquiry into the Wealth of Nations*, by Adam Smith, 1776. (This version taken from the Modern Library edition, 1937).

interest to employ him, unless he was to share in the produce of his labour, or unless his stock was to be replaced to him with a profit. This profit makes a second deduction from the produce of the labour which is employed upon land.

The produce of almost all other labour is liable to [similar] deduction of profit. In all arts and manufactures the greater part of the workmen stand in need of a master to advance them the materials of their work, and their wages and maintenance till it be compleated. He shares in the produce of their labour, or in the value which it adds to the materials upon which it is bestowed; and in this share consists his profit.

It sometimes happens, indeed, that a single independent workman has stock sufficient both to purchase the materials of his work, and to maintain himself till it be compleated. He is both master and workman, and enjoys the whole produce of his own labour, or the whole value which it adds to the materials upon which it is bestowed. It includes what are usually two distinct revenues, belonging to two distinct persons, the profits of stock, and the wage of labour.

Such cases, however, are not very frequent, and in every part of Europe, twenty workmen serve under a master for one that is independent; and the wages of labour are every where understood to be, what they usually are, when the labourer is one person, and the owner of the stock which employs him another.

What . . . the common wages of labour [amount to], depends every where upon the contract usually made between those two parties, whose interests are by no means the same. The workmen desire to get as much, the masters to give as little as possible. The former are disposed to combine [join together] in order to raise, the latter in order to lower the wages of labour.

It is not, however, difficult to foresee which of the two parties must, upon all ordinary occasions, have the advantage in the dispute, and force the other into a compliance with their terms. The masters, being fewer in number, can combine much more easily; and the law, besides, authorises, or at least does not prohibit their combinations, while it prohibits those of the workmen. We have no acts of parliament against combining to lower the price of work; but many against combining to raise it. In all such disputes the masters can hold out much longer. A landlord, a farmer, a master manufacturer, or merchant, though they did not employ a single workman, could generally live a year or two upon the stocks which they have already acquired. Many workmen could not subsist a week, few could subsist a month, and scarce any a year without employment. In the long-run the workman may be as necessary to his master as his master is to him, but the necessity is not so immediate.

1787–1799

CHAPTER 2

SHAYS'S REBELLION

HOWARD ZINN

Although it is commonly believed that America returned to peace after the Revolutionary War in 1783, poor farmers in western Massachusetts were quite unhappy with the new government. In fact, they could find little difference between their former British rulers and the wealthy American businessmen who came to power after the war.

During the 1780s the Massachusetts government, led by wealthy merchants, imposed heavy taxes on its citizens to pay off debts accumulated during the war. By 1786, the government was seizing property from hundreds of farmers who could not pay their taxes. Some were put into debtors' prison. In August a violent uprising attempted to close down courts where orders for land seizures were issued.

Known as Shays's Rebellion for its leader, Daniel Shays, the revolt was not nearly as bloody as the American Revolution. But the uprising inspired the founding fathers to initiate the first Constitutional Convention in order to form a powerful national government that could tax all citizens for war debts and quash such rebellions in the future.

Howard Zinn is a best-selling author whose books focus on the influence of historical events on average people. *A People's History of the United States* has sold over five hundred thousand copies and is used to teach American history in many countries around the world.

To many Americans over the years, the Constitution drawn up in 1787 has seemed a work of genius put together by wise, humane men who created a legal framework for democracy and equality. This view is stated, a bit extravagantly, by the historian George Bancroft, writing in the early nineteenth century:

> The Constitution establishes nothing that interferes with equality and individuality. It knows nothing of differences by descent, or opinions, of favored classes, or legalized religion, or the political power of property. It leaves the individual alongside of the individual. . . . As the sea is made up of drops, American society is composed of separate, free, and constantly moving atoms, ever in reciprocal action . . . so that the institutions and laws of the country rise out of the masses of individual thought which, like the waters of the ocean, are rolling evermore.

Another view of the Constitution was put forward early in the twentieth century by the historian Charles Beard (arousing anger and indignation, including a denunciatory editorial in the *New York Times*). He wrote in his book *An Economic Interpretation of the Constitution:*

> Inasmuch as the primary object of a government, beyond the mere repression of physical violence, is the making of the rules which determine the property relations of members of society, the dominant classes whose rights are thus to be determined must perforce obtain from the government such rules as are consonant with the larger interests necessary to the continuance of their economic processes, or they must themselves control the organs of government.

In short, Beard said, the rich must, in their own interest, either control the government directly or control the laws by which government operates.

Beard applied this general idea to the Constitution, by studying the economic backgrounds and political ideas of the fifty-five men who gathered in Philadelphia in 1787 to draw up the Constitution. He found that a majority of them were lawyers by profession, that most of them were men of wealth, in land, slaves, manufacturing, or shipping, that half of them had money loaned out at interest, and that forty of the fifty-five held government bonds, according to the records of the Treasury Department.

Thus, Beard found that most of the makers of the Constitution had some direct economic interest in establishing a strong federal government: the manufacturers needed protective tariffs; the moneylenders wanted to stop the use of paper money to pay off debts; the land speculators wanted protection as they invaded Indian lands; slaveowners needed federal security against slave revolts and runaways; bondholders wanted a government able to raise money by nationwide taxation, to pay off those bonds.

Four groups, Beard noted, were not represented in the Constitutional Convention: slaves, indentured servants, women, men without property. And so the Constitution did not reflect the interests of those groups.

He wanted to make it clear that he did not think the Constitution was written merely to benefit the Founding Fathers personally, although one could not ignore the $150,000 fortune of Benjamin Franklin, the connections of Alexander Hamilton to wealthy interests through his father-in-law and brother-in-law, the great slave plantations of James Madison, the enormous landholdings of George Washington. Rather, it was to benefit the groups the Founders represented, the "economic interests they understood and felt in concrete, definite form through their own personal experience."

Not everyone at the Philadelphia Convention fitted Beard's scheme. Elbridge Gerry of Massachusetts was a holder of landed property, and yet he opposed the ratification of the Constitution. Similarly, Luther Martin of Maryland, whose ancestors had obtained large tracts of land in New Jersey, opposed ratification. But, with a few exceptions, Beard found a strong connection between wealth and support of the Constitution.

FARMERS REVOLT

By 1787 there was not only a positive need for strong central government to protect the large economic interests, but also immediate fear of rebellion by discontented farmers. The chief event causing this fear was an uprising in the summer of 1786 in western Massachusetts, known as Shays' Rebellion.

In the western towns of Massachusetts there was resentment against the legislature in Boston. The new Constitution of 1780 had raised the property qualifications for voting. No one could hold state office without being quite wealthy. Furthermore, the legislature was refusing to issue paper money, as had been done in some other states, like Rhode Island, to make it easier for debt-ridden farmers to pay off their creditors.

Illegal conventions began to assemble in some of the western counties to organize opposition to the legislature. At one of these, a man named Plough Jogger spoke his mind:

> I have been greatly abused, have been obliged to do more than my part in the war; been loaded with class rates [taxes], town rates, province rates, Continental rates and all rates . . . been pulled and hauled by sheriffs, constables and collectors, and had my cattle sold

for less than they were worth. . . .

> The great men are going to get all we have and I think
> it is time for us to rise and put a stop to it, and have no
> more courts, nor sheriffs, nor collectors nor lawyers. . . .

The chairman of that meeting used his gavel to cut short the applause. He and others wanted to redress their grievances, but peacefully, by petition to the General Court (the legislature) in Boston.

However, before the scheduled meeting of the General Court, there were going to be court proceedings in Hampshire County, in the towns of Northampton and Springfield, to seize the cattle of farmers who hadn't paid their debts, to take away their land, now full of grain and ready for harvest. And so, veterans of the Continental army, also aggrieved because they had been treated poorly on discharge—given certificates for future redemption instead of immediate cash—began to organize the farmers into squads and companies. One of these veterans was Luke Day, who arrived the morning of court with a fife-and-drum corps, still angry with the memory of being locked up in debtors' prison in the heat of the previous summer.

The sheriff looked to the local militia to defend the court against these armed farmers. But most of the militia was with Luke Day. The sheriff did manage to gather five hundred men, and the judges put on their black silk robes, waiting for the sheriff to protect their trip to the courthouse. But there at the courthouse steps, Luke Day stood with a petition, asserting the people's constitutional right to protest the unconstitutional acts of the General Court, asking the judges to adjourn until the General Court could act on behalf of the farmers. Standing with Luke Day were fifteen hundred armed farmers. The judges adjourned.

WIDESPREAD PROTEST

Shortly after, at courthouses in Worcester and Athol, farmers with guns prevented the courts from meeting to take away their property, and the militia were too sympathetic to the farmers, or too outnumbered, to act. In Concord, a fifty-year-old veteran of two wars, Job Shattuck, led a caravan of carts, wagons, horses, and oxen onto the town green, while a message was sent to the judges:

> The voice of the People of this county is such that the
> court shall not enter this courthouse until such time as
> the People shall have redress of the grievances they la-
> bor under at the present.

A county convention then suggested the judges adjourn, which they did.

At Great Barrington, a militia of a thousand faced a square crowded with armed men and boys. But the militia was split in its opinion. When the chief justice suggested the militia divide, those in favor of the court's sitting to go on the right side of the road, and those against on the left, two hundred of the militia went to the right, eight hundred to the left, and the judges adjourned. Then the crowd went to the home of the chief justice, who agreed to sign a pledge that the court would not sit until the Massachusetts General Court met. The crowd went back to the square, broke open the county jail, and set free the debtors. The chief justice, a country doctor, said: "I have never heard anybody point out a better way to have their grievances redressed than the people have taken."

The governor and the political leaders of Massachusetts became alarmed. Samuel Adams, once looked on as a radical leader in Boston, now insisted people act within the law. He said "British emissaries" were stirring up the farmers. People in the town of Greenwich responded: You in Boston have the money, and we don't. And didn't you act illegally yourselves in the Revolution? The insurgents were now being called Regulators. Their emblem was a sprig of hemlock.

The problem went beyond Massachusetts. In Rhode Island, the debtors had taken over the legislature and were issuing paper money. In New Hampshire, several hundred men, in September of 1786, surrounded the legislature in Exeter, asking that taxes be returned and paper money issued; they dispersed only when military action was threatened.

SHAYS' REBELLION

Daniel Shays entered the scene in western Massachusetts. A poor farm hand when the revolution broke out, he joined the Continental army, fought at Lexington, Bunker Hill, and Saratoga, and was wounded in action. In 1780, not being paid, he resigned from the army, went home, and soon found himself in court for nonpayment of debts. He also saw what was happening to others: a sick woman, unable to pay, had her bed taken from under her.

What brought Shays fully into the situation was that on September 19, the Supreme Judicial Court of Massachusetts met in Worcester and indicted eleven leaders of the rebellion, including three of his friends, as "disorderly, riotous and seditious persons" who "unlawfully and by force of arms" prevented "the execution of justice and the laws of the commonwealth." The Supreme Judicial Court planned to meet again in Springfield a week later, and there was talk of Luke Day's being indicted.

Shays organized seven hundred armed farmers, most of them

veterans of the war, and led them to Springfield. There they found a general with nine hundred soldiers and a cannon. Shays asked the general for permission to parade, which the general granted, so Shays and his men moved through the square, drums banging and fifes blowing. As they marched, their ranks grew. Some of the militia joined, and reinforcements began coming in from the countryside. The judges postponed hearings for a day, then adjourned the court.

Now the General Court, meeting in Boston, was told by Governor James Bowdoin to "vindicate the insulted dignity of government." The recent rebels against England, secure in office, were calling for law and order. Sam Adams helped draw up a Riot Act, and a resolution suspending habeas corpus, to allow the authorities to keep people in jail without trial. At the same time, the legislature moved to make some concessions to the angry farmers, saying certain old taxes could now be paid in goods instead of money.

This didn't help. In Worcester, 160 insurgents appeared at the courthouse. The sheriff read the Riot Act. The insurgents said they would disperse only if the judges did. The sheriff shouted something about hanging. Someone came up behind him and put a sprig of [poisonous] hemlock in his hat. The judges left.

Confrontations between farmers and militia now multiplied. The winter snows began to interfere with the trips of farmers to the courthouses. When Shays began marching a thousand men into Boston, a blizzard forced them back, and one of his men froze to death.

An army came into the field, led by General Benjamin Lincoln, on money raised by Boston merchants. In an artillery duel, three rebels were killed. One soldier stepped in front of his own artillery piece and lost both arms. The winter grew worse. The rebels were outnumbered and on the run. Shays took refuge in Vermont, and his followers began to surrender. There were a few more deaths in battle, and then sporadic, disorganized, desperate acts of violence against authority: the burning of barns, the slaughter of a general's horses. One government soldier was killed in an eerie night-time collision of two sleighs.

CONDEMNED TO DEATH

Captured rebels were put on trial in Northampton and six were sentenced to death. A note was left at the door of the high sheriff of Pittsfield:

> I understand that there is a number of my countrymen
> condemned to die because they fought for justice. I
> pray have a care that you assist not in the execution of

so horrid a crime, for by all that is above, he that condemns and he that executes shall share alike. . . . Prepare for death with speed, for your life or mine is short.
When the woods are covered with leaves, I shall return
and pay you a short visit.

Thirty-three more rebels were put on trial and six more condemned to death. Arguments took place over whether the hangings should go forward. General Lincoln urged mercy and a
Commission of Clemency, but Samuel Adams said: "In monarchy the crime of treason may admit of being pardoned or lightly
punished, but the man who dares rebel against the laws of a republic ought to suffer death." Several hangings followed; some
of the condemned were pardoned. Shays, in Vermont, was pardoned in 1788 and returned to Massachusetts, where he died,
poor and obscure, in 1825.

PERSUADING THE STATES TO UNITE

JOHN JAY

John Jay, one of the founding fathers of the United States and a signer the Declaration of Independence, was the New York delegate to the Continental Congress and later became the first chief justice to the Supreme Court. Jay was an early advocate for a strong federal government but was opposed by many New Yorkers. To convince voters to ratify the Constitution, Jay wrote five of the eighty-five essays known collectively as *The Federalist*, which were published in New York newspapers between 1787 and 1788. In the following excerpt, Jay reminds New Yorkers that they share a common bond with the citizens who live in the other twelve American states.

To the People of the State of New York:
When the people of America reflect that they are now called upon to decide a question, which, in its consequences, must prove one of the most important, that ever engaged their attention, the propriety of their taking a very comprehensive, as well as a very serious, view of it, will be evident.

Nothing is more certain than the indispensable necessity of Government, and it is equally undeniable, that whenever and however it is instituted, the people must cede to it some of their natural rights, in order to vest it with requisite powers. It is well worthy of consideration, therefore, whether . . . the people of America, should . . . be one nation, under one Fœderal Government, or . . . should divide themselves into separate confederacies, and give to the head of each, the same kind of powers which

From *The Federalist*, nos. 1 and 2, by John Jay, in *American Historical Documents, 1000–1904*, edited by Charles W. Eliot (New York: Collier, 1910).

they are advised to place in one national Government.

It has until lately been a received and uncontradicted opinion, that the prosperity of the people of America depended on their continuing firmly united, and the wishes, prayers, and efforts of our best and wisest Citizens have been constantly directed to that object. But Politicians now appear, who insist that this opinion is erroneous, and that instead of looking for safety and happiness in union, we ought to seek it in a division of the States into distinct confederacies or sovereignties. However extraordinary this new doctrine may appear, it nevertheless has its advocates. . . . Whatever may be the arguments or inducements which have wrought this change in the sentiments and declarations of these Gentlemen, it certainly would not be wise in the people at large to adopt these new political tenets without being fully convinced that they are founded in truth and sound Policy.

ONE UNITED PEOPLE

It has often given me pleasure to observe, that Independent America was not composed of detached and distant territories, but that one connected, fertile, wide-spreading country was the [estate] of our western sons of liberty. Providence has in a particular manner blessed it with a variety of soils and productions and watered it with innumerable streams, for the delight and accommodation of its inhabitants. A succession of navigable waters forms a kind of chain round its borders, as if to bind it together; while the most noble rivers in the world, running at convenient distances, present them with highways for the easy communication of friendly aids, and the mutual transportation and exchange of their various commodities.

With equal pleasure I have as often taken notice, that Providence has been pleased to give this one connected country, to one united people; a people descended from the same ancestors, speaking the same language, professing the same religion, attached to the same principles of government, very similar in their manners and customs, and who, by their joint counsels, arms and efforts, fighting side by side throughout a long and bloody war, have nobly established their general Liberty and Independence.

This country and this people seem to have been made for each other, and it appears as if it was the design of Providence, that an inheritance so proper and convenient for a band of brethren, united to each other by the strongest ties, should never be split into a number of unsocial, jealous, and alien sovereignties.

Similar sentiments have hitherto prevailed among all orders and denominations of men among us. To all general purposes we have uniformly been one people; each individual citizen everywhere enjoying the same national rights, privileges, and protection. As a nation we have made peace and war: as a nation we have vanquished our common enemies: as a nation we have formed alliances and made treaties, and entered into various compacts and conventions with foreign States.

A strong sense of the value and blessings of Union induced the people, at a very early period, to institute a Fœderal Government to preserve and perpetuate it. They formed it almost as soon as they had a political existence; nay, at a time, when their habitations were in flames, when many of their Citizens were bleeding, and when the progress of hostility and desolation left little room for those calm and mature inquiries and reflections, which must ever precede the formation of a wise and well-balanced government for a free people. It is not to be wondered at, that a Government instituted in times so inauspicious, should on experiment be found greatly deficient and inadequate to the purpose it was intended to answer.

THE CONSTITUTIONAL CONVENTION

This intelligent people perceived and regretted these defects. Still continuing no less attached to Union, than enamored of Liberty, they observed the danger, which immediately threatened the former and more remotely the latter; and being persuaded that ample security for both, could only be found in a national Government more wisely framed, they, as with one voice, convened the late Convention at Philadelphia, to take that important subject under consideration.

This Convention, composed of men who possessed the confidence of the people, and many of whom had become highly distinguished by their patriotism, virtue, and wisdom, in times which tried the minds and hearts of men, undertook the arduous task. In the mild season of peace, with minds unoccupied by other subjects, they passed many months in cool, uninterrupted, and daily consultations; and finally, without having been awed by power, or influenced by any passions except love for their Country, they presented and recommended to the people the plan produced by their joint and very unanimous councils.

Admit, for so is the fact, that this plan is only *recommended*, not imposed, yet let it be remembered that it is . . . recommended . . . to that sedate and candid consideration, which the magnitude and importance of the subject demand, and which it certainly ought to receive. But this . . . is more to be wished than expected, that it may be so considered and examined. Experience on a former occasion teaches us not to be too [optimistic] in such hopes. It is not yet forgotten, that well grounded apprehensions of imminent danger induced the people of America to form the Memorable Congress of 1774. That Body recommended certain measures to their Constituents, and the event proved their wisdom; yet it is fresh in our memories how soon the Press began to teem with Pamphlets and weekly Papers against those very measures. Not only many of the Officers of Government, who obeyed the dictates of personal interest, but others, from a mistaken estimate of consequences, or the undue influence of former attachments, or whose ambition aimed at objects which did not correspond with the public good, were indefatigable in their endeavors to persuade the people to reject the advice of that Patriotic Congress. Many indeed were deceived and deluded, but the great majority of the people reasoned and decided judiciously; and happy they are in reflecting that they did so.

They considered that the Congress was composed of many wise and experienced men. That being convened from different parts of the country they brought with them and communicated to each other a variety of useful information. That in the course of the time they passed together in inquiring into and discussing the true interests of their country, they must have acquired very accurate knowledge on that head. That they were individually interested in the public liberty and prosperity, and therefore that it was not less their inclination than their duty, to recommend only such measures as after the most mature deliberation they really thought prudent and advisable.

These and similar considerations then induced the people to rely greatly on the judgment and integrity of the Congress; and they took their advice, notwithstanding the various arts and endeavors used to deter and dissuade them from it. But if the people at large had reason to confide in the men of that Congress, few of whom had then been fully tried or generally known, still greater reason have they now to respect the judgment and advice of the Convention, for it is well known that some of the most distinguished members of that Congress, who have been since tried and justly approved for patriotism and abilities, and who have grown old in acquiring political information, were also members of this Convention, and carried into it their accumulated knowledge and experience.

It is worthy of remark, that not only the first, but every succeeding Congress, as well as the late Convention, have invariably joined with the people in thinking that the prosperity of America depended on its Union. To preserve and perpetuate it, was the great object of the people in forming that Convention, and it is also the great object of the plan which the Convention has advised them to adopt. With what propriety, therefore, or for what good purposes, are attempts at this particular period, made by some men, to depreciate the importance of the Union? Or why is it suggested that three or four confederacies would be better than one? I am persuaded in my own mind, that the people have always thought right on this subject, and that their universal and uniform attachment to the cause of the Union rests on great and weighty reasons, which I shall endeavor to develop and explain in some ensuing papers. They who promote the idea of substituting a number of distinct confederacies in the room of the plan of the Convention, seem clearly to foresee that the rejection of it would put the continuance of the Union in the utmost jeopardy: that certainly would be the case, and I sincerely wish that it may be as clearly foreseen by every good Citizen, that whenever the dissolution of the Union arrives, America will have reason to exclaim in the words of the Poet [Publius], "Farewell! A Long Farewell, to All My Greatness."

THE BILL OF RIGHTS

JAMES MADISON

Americans in the original thirteen states were reluctant to assign authority to a powerful federal government unless certain basic liberties could be guaranteed. James Madison agreed and drafted the Bill of Rights, ten amendments to the U.S. Constitution that limited federal powers and favored individual liberty. The First Congress voted to add the Bill of Rights to the Constitution on September 25, 1789. With these individual rights so defined, eleven state legislatures adopted the U.S. Constitution by 1791, and the Bill of Rights became law.

The ten rights secured in the document were used as a basis for the French Declaration of the Rights of Man and Citizen, which was adopted during the 1789 French Revolution. Since that time the U.S. Bill of Rights has provided a model for democratic revolutionaries and constitutional democracies throughout the world.

Amendment I. Congress shall make no law respecting an establishment of religion, or prohibiting the free exercise thereof; or abridging the freedom of speech, or of the press; or the right of the people peaceably to assemble, and to petition the Government for a redress of grievances.

Amendment II. A well regulated Militia, being necessary to the security of a free State, the right of the people to keep and bear Arms, shall not be infringed.

Amendment III. No Soldier shall, in time of peace be quartered in any house, without the consent of the Owner, nor in time of war, but in a manner to be prescribed by law.

Amendment IV. The right of the people to be secure in their persons, houses, papers, and effects, against unreasonable

The U.S. Bill of Rights (National Archives and Records Administration, Washington, D.C.).

searches and seizures, shall not be violated, and no Warrants shall issue, but upon probable cause, supported by Oath or affirmation, and particularly describing the place to be searched, and the persons or things to be seized.

Amendment V. No person shall be held to answer for a capital, or otherwise infamous crime, unless on a presentment or indictment of a Grand Jury, except in cases arising in the land or naval forces, or in the Militia, when in actual service in time of War or public danger; nor shall any person be subject for the same offence to be twice put in jeopardy of life or limb; nor shall be compelled in any criminal case to be a witness against himself, nor be deprived of life, liberty, or property, without due process of law; nor shall private property be taken for public use, without just compensation.

Amendment VI. In all criminal prosecutions, the accused shall enjoy the right to a speedy and public trial, by an impartial jury of the State and district wherein the crime shall have been committed, which district shall have been previously ascertained by law, and to be informed of the nature and cause of the accusation; to be confronted with the witnesses against him; to have compulsory process for obtaining witnesses in his favor, and to have the Assistance of Counsel for his defense.

Amendment VII. In suits at common law, where the value in controversy shall exceed twenty dollars, the right of trial by jury shall be preserved, and no fact tried by a jury, shall be otherwise reexamined in any Court of the United States, than according to the rules of the common law.

Amendment VIII. Excessive bail shall not be required, nor excessive fines imposed, nor cruel and unusual punishments inflicted.

Amendment IX. The enumeration in the Constitution, of certain rights, shall not be construed to deny or disparage others retained by the people.

Amendment X. The powers not delegated to the United States by the Constitution, nor prohibited by it to the States, are reserved to the States respectively, or to the people.

REVOLUTION ON BOTH SIDES OF THE ATLANTIC

JACQUES GODECHOT

In the last quarter of the eighteenth century, farmers, peasants and a large number of professionals and businessmen fomented violent revolution on both sides of the Atlantic Ocean. Beginning with the first shots of the Revolutionary War in 1775, disorganized armies of poor and middle-class workers upset powerful monarchies from America to France to Russia. Although most European revolts did not realize long-term success, the seeds of freedom had been planted and would eventually take hold in much of the Western Hemisphere.

In the 1960s historian Jacques Godechot popularized the theory that this revolutionary climate found its inspiration in the commonly held political beliefs that promoted individual freedom and equal rights.

I n 1763 the era of great social movements was long past. There had been no major civil war for many decades, not since the wars of religion of the late sixteenth and early seventeenth centuries. . . . Thereafter the people lived so quietly and obediently under the rule of emperors, kings, and republics that there appeared no prospect that the social movements would be renewed. . . .

REVOLUTIONARY UPRISING

But around 1770 a force was released which the governments were no longer accustomed to dealing with. This was the crowd,

Reprinted and edited with permission of The Free Press, a division of Simon & Schuster, Inc., from *France and the Atlantic Revolution of the Eighteenth Century, 1770–1799,* by Jacques Godechot, translated by Herbert A. Rowen. Copyright © 1965 by The Free Press.

the mass of ordinary people. Riots and popular uprisings began to occur everywhere in the Western world from the Urals [in Russia] to the Alleghenies [in America], often with very dissimilar causes and apparently very unrelated goals. These outbreaks were especially violent along the Atlantic coasts, especially in North America, France, and the Netherlands. . . .

The revolutionary movement began in 1768 in the republic of Geneva, a tiny corner of Western Europe wedged between France, the Swiss Confederation, and the kingdom of Sardinia. Agitation arose among the poor "natives" *(natifs)*, persons born in Geneva of immigrant parents of foreign nationality. Following the advice of their celebrated compatriot [philosopher] Jean-Jacques Rousseau in his *Social Contract*, published six years before, they demanded equality of rights with the citizens.

During 1768 agitation also began in the English colonies of North America. The colonists were aroused by measures taken by the British government regarding Canada and Louisiana, by new taxes, and by the attitude of King George III of England, who apparently wished to govern his American subjects in all things without consulting their representatives. The Boston Massacre, the first armed conflict, occurred in 1770. It was followed three years later by another popular disturbance, the Boston Tea Party. In 1775 came the battles of Lexington and Concord between colonial insurgents and His Britannic Majesty's army. Civil war was soon transformed into international war, which ended only eight years later with the recognition of the independence of the United States of America.

But 1775 was the year not only of the American uprising. During the same year two other insurrections took place, at opposite ends of Europe. Although both were peasant rebellions, there was no visible connection between them. One was the great uprising of Russian peasants known as the Pugachev Revolt, which lasted from 1773 to 1775; the other was the peasant revolt in the Paris region which has remained celebrated under the name of the Flour War *(guerre des farines)*.

DEMANDING SOCIAL STATUS

Three years later disorders broke out in Ireland in connection with the demands of the Irish Volunteers, a movement at first limited to Protestants but soon extended to Catholics. Like the "natives" of Geneva, the serfs of Russia, and the American colonists, the Irish demanded a change in their status in society. The agitation of the Irish caused disorders within England by contagion and by reaction. These were the Yorkshire Movement and especially the frightful Gordon Riots in London during June

1780. During the Gordon Riots, some fifty houses were burned down, more than were lost by similar violence in Paris during the entire period of the revolution. A few concessions by the British Parliament, but even more the end of the war in America, brought the agitation in Great Britain to a halt. But the revolution was rekindled in Geneva at the same moment. The "natives," unable to gain victory in 1768, seized power with the aid of the "burghers" (bourgeois) in April 1782 and attempted to give the old republic a new and more democratic constitution. They failed as a result of the intervention of French, Sardinian, Bernese, and Zurich troops called in by the aristocrats.

This setback did not discourage the Dutch burghers, who began an insurrection in 1783 against the stadholder, the leader of the United Provinces. Like the Genevans, they were victorious after four years of struggle, but they too had to face foreign troops. Prussian soldiers and British sailors called in by the stadholder entered the Dutch Republic in 1787 and reestablished the old regime.

In spite of what had happened in Geneva and Amsterdam, the Belgians did not hesitate to revolt against their sovereign, Emperor Joseph II, in 1787. The Belgian "Patriots" were victorious in 1789, but they unfortunately were split between liberals (Vonckists) and conservatives (Statists). They too had to accept defeat when faced by intervention of Austrian troops the following year.

THE FRENCH REVOLUTION SPREADS

In the midst of these events, revolution broke out in France. It began with a revolt of the nobility in 1787. When elections to the Estates General were held in 1789, the revolution spread to every stratum of the nation, especially to the peasantry, who constituted 90 percent of the population. In France the revolution was deeper and more violent than anywhere else in the West. This is why for so long it has been customary to speak of the "French Revolution" even when what is meant are all social and political movements which disturbed Europe from 1787 to 1815. The revolution in France not only toppled the old regime and replaced it by a new order in that country; it also rekindled and fed the flame of revolution, and bore it to other parts of the world. First was Poland, where King Stanislas Poniatowski carried through a true political revolution on May 3, 1791, with the aid of the bourgeoisie and a fraction of the "enlightened" nobility. Poland was drawn into new wars with its neighbors and a more democratic revolution in 1794, but the price it paid was defeat and the partition of the remaining Polish territory among Russia, Prussia, and Austria in 1795.

The revolution in France gave new hope to the refugee revolutionaries from Geneva, Holland, Belgium, and Ireland. In France they reasserted and strengthened their beliefs, and formed military units in preparation for resuming their interrupted work. The revolution broke out again in 1792 in Switzerland, at Geneva, and at Porrentruy. . . . In the same year Belgian revolutionaries returning home upon the heels of the French troops renewed their attack on the old regime in the Austrian Netherlands. A revolution broke out in 1790 in the Comtat Venaissin and Avignon, papal possessions enclaved in southern France, and these territories joined France the next year. Savoy imitated them in 1792. During the same year the Rhineland also displayed its sympathies for the revolution. In 1795 Dutch revolutionaries following after invading French troops were able to return to Holland where they organized a democratic republic. The following year it was Italy which was reached by the revolution; in 1798 it was all of Switzerland; and in 1799 the revolutionary ideas were carried by French armies to Malta and Egypt. England and Ireland were not spared disorder. Only the vigorous action of the British government prevented the revolutionary movement from spreading in England and overthrowing its authority in Ireland. Although by 1799 the revolutionary ideas had gained adherents everywhere in the West, there were countries—Russia, Scandinavia, the Ottoman Empire, Spain, and Portugal—where they had very little broad influence.

The year 1799 marked a stage in the course of the revolution, not its end. The spread of revolutionary ideas did not end when a military dictator came to power in France in the person of Napoleon Bonaparte. The soldiers of the [French] Consulate and the Empire carried the revolutionary doctrines to regions where they had as yet hardly penetrated—Hungary, Russia, the South of Spain, and Portugal. From Iberia they were carried to Spanish and Portuguese America. The war of independence of the Spanish colonies in America was an integral part of the revolutionary movement. But after 1799 a change took place in the methods by which the revolution spread. No longer was there vigorous activity by the mass of the people. . . .

The three decades from 1770 to 1800 were marked by revolutionary disorders, in contrast to the calm and the popular submissiveness which had characterized the previous seventy years. Yet it is possible to hold that all these revolutionary disorders were the result only of mere coincidence. To prove that they actually belonged to a single great movement and formed a single Atlantic Revolution we must prove that they arose from identical general causes.

THE CAUSES OF THE ATLANTIC REVOLUTION

Causes common to a revolutionary movement extending over half of Europe and the European-colonized part of America necessarily lay very deep in the character of society. In the first place, these causes were certainly bound up with transformations in the social structure itself. This was asserted in 1793 by Barnave, a French revolutionary and former member of the Constituent Assembly, who died later that year on the guillotine. In an interesting book, *Introduction to the French Revolution, . . .* Barnave showed that everywhere in Europe society had been originally feudal, with the immense majority of inhabitants living under the domination of the landed aristocracy. Possession of the land had been the only source of wealth and the basis of power. The great discoveries of [the New World in] the sixteenth century and the rise of transoceanic navigation led to development of a new social class, the commercial bourgeoisie, and to the growth of great cities, in particular the ports situated on either side of the ocean—London, Paris, Rouen, Antwerp, Amsterdam, Hamburg, New York, and Philadelphia.

The commercial bourgeoisie of these great cities spurred the expansion of industry, which became very rapid after the late eighteenth century thanks to the invention of the steam engine and other machines. The labor force expanded rapidly too. The revolution originated ultimately in the desire of the new classes, especially the bourgeoisie, to come to power. Nor, declared Barnave, was the revolution limited to a single country; it was a "European revolution with France at its apex."

Present-day historians, recognizing the truth of Barnave's ideas . . . regret, however, that Barnave spoke of a purely "European" revolution, for the revolutionary movement first showed its force across the Atlantic. It would be better to speak either of the "Revolution of the West" or of the "Atlantic Revolution."

CAUSES OF THE FRENCH REVOLUTION

WILL DURANT AND ARIEL DURANT

The French Revolution, which took place between 1789 and 1799, was a violent and bloody revolt that caused a king and his wife to lose their heads, launched a reign of terror that killed thousands, and inspired similar uprisings in almost every European country from Italy to Russia. The causes of the revolution were many, including a weak monarch, a free-spending religious hierarchy that owned one-fifth of the land, a do-nothing nobility that owned another quarter, and a highly taxed peasantry that made up a large majority of the French populace.

As Will and Ariel Durant explain, these problems were magnified after natural disasters and poor grain harvests enhanced peoples' discontent with their ruler.

Will Durant was born in 1885 and, after teaching college in New York, began working up to fourteen hours a day in order to write the definitive ten-volume History of Civilization series with the help of his wife, Ariel. Beginning in 1927, the Durants traveled around the world writing and researching until the last volume of the series was completed in 1967.

[W]ith 25 million people] France was the most populous and prosperous nation in Europe . . . in 1780. . . . Paris was the largest city in Europe, with some 650,000 inhabitants, the best-educated and most excitable in Europe.

The people of France were divided into three orders, or classes (*états*—states or estates): the clergy, some 130,000 souls; the nobility, some 400,000; and the Tiers État [Third Estate], which in-

Reprinted with the permission of Simon & Schuster, from *The Age of Napoleon*, by Will and Ariel Durant. Copyright © 1975 by Will and Ariel Durant.

cluded everybody else; the Revolution was the attempt of this economically rising but politically disadvantaged Third Estate to achieve political power and social acceptance [equal to] its growing wealth. Each of the classes was divided into subgroups or layers, so that nearly everyone could enjoy the sight of persons below him.

The richest class was the ecclesiastical hierarchy—cardinals, archbishops, bishops, and abbots; among the poorest were the pastors and curates of the countryside; here the economic factor crossed the lines of doctrine, and in the Revolution the lower clergy joined with the [common people] against their own superiors. Monastic life had lost its lure. . . . Religion in general had declined in the French cities; in many towns the churches were half empty; and among the peasantry pagan customs and old superstitions competed actively with the doctrines and ceremonies of the Church. The nuns, however, were still actively devoted to teaching and nursing, and were honored by rich and poor alike. . . .

A POWERFUL CLERGY

The state supported the Church because statesmen generally agreed that the clergy gave them indispensable aid in preserving social order. In their view the natural inequality of human endowment made inevitable an unequal distribution of wealth; it seemed important, for the safety of the possessing classes, that a corps of clerics should be maintained to provide the poor with counsels of peaceful humility and expectation of . . . Paradise. It meant much to France that the family, buttressed with religion, remained as the basis of national stability through all vicissitudes of the state. Moreover, obedience was encouraged by belief in the divine right of kings—the divine origin of their appointment and power; the clergy [taught] this belief, and the kings felt that this myth was a precious aid to their personal security and orderly rule. . . .

Grateful for these services, the state allowed the Church to collect tithes and other income from each parish, and to manage the making of wills—which encouraged . . . sinners to buy promissory notes, collectible in heaven, in exchange for earthly property bequeathed to the Church. The government exempted the clergy from taxation, and contented itself with receiving, now and then, a substantial . . . free grant from the Church. So variously privileged, the Church in France accumulated large domains, reckoned by some as a fifth of the soil; and these it ruled as feudal properties, collecting feudal dues. It turned the contributions of the faithful into gold and silver ornaments which, like the jewels of the crown, were consecrated and inviolable hedges against the inflation that seemed ingrained in history.

Many parish priests . . . labored in pious poverty, while many bishops lived in stately elegance, and lordly archbishops . . . fluttered about the court of the king. As the French government neared bankruptcy, while the French Church . . . enjoyed an annual income of [approximately $450] million . . . the tax-burdened Third Estate wondered why the Church should not be compelled to share its wealth with the state. When the literature of unbelief spread, thousands of middle-class citizens and hundreds of aristocrats shed the Christian faith, and were ready to view with philosophic calm the raids of the Revolution upon the sacred, guarded hoard.

THE CORRUPT NOBILITY

The nobility was vaguely conscious that it had outlived many of the functions that had been its reasons for being. Its proudest element, the nobility of the sword (*noblesse d'épée*), had served as the military guard, economic director, and judiciary head of the agricultural communities; but much of these services had been superseded by the centralization of power and administration under [Cardinal] Richelieu and Louis XIV; many of the seigneurs now lived at the court and neglected their domains; and their rich raiment, fine manners, and general amiability seemed, in 1789, insufficient reason for owning a fourth of the soil and exacting feudal dues. . . .

A rising portion of the aristocracy—the *noblesse de robe,* or nobility of the gown—consisted of some four thousand families whose heads had been appointed to judicial or administrative posts that automatically endowed their holders with nobility. As most such posts had been sold by the king or his ministers to raise revenue for the state, many of the purchasers felt warranted in regaining their outlay by . . . bribes; "venality in office" was "unusually widespread in France," and was one of a hundred complaints against the dying regime. Some of these titles to office and rank were hereditary, and as their holders multiplied, especially in the *parlements,* or law courts, of the various districts, their pride and power grew to the point where in 1787 the Parlement of Paris claimed the right to veto the decrees of the king. In terms of time the Revolution began near the top.

EVERYTHING, NOTHING, AND SOMETHING

In *Qu'est-ce que le Tiers état?*—a pamphlet published in January, 1780—the Abbé Emmanuel-Joseph Sieyès asked and answered three questions: What is the Third Estate? Everything. What has it been till now? Nothing. What does it want to be? Something.

. . . It was nearly everything. It included the bourgeoisie, or middle class, with its 100,000 families and its many layers—bankers, brokers, manufacturers, merchants, managers, lawyers, physicians, scientists, teachers, artists, authors, journalists, the press (the fourth "estate," or power); and the *menu peuple,* "little people" (sometimes called "the people"), consisting of the proletariat and tradesmen of the towns, the transport workers on land or sea, and the peasantry.

The upper middle classes held and managed a rising and spreading force: the power of mobile money and other capital in aggressive, expansive competition with the power of static land or a declining creed. They speculated on the stock exchanges of Paris, London, and Amsterdam, and . . . controlled half the money of Europe. They financed the French government with loans, and threatened to overthrow it if their loans and charges were not met. They owned or managed the rapidly developing mining and metallurgical industry of northern France, the textile industry of Lyons, Troyes, Abbeville, Lille, and Rouen, the iron and salt works of Lorraine, the soap factories of Marseilles, the tanneries of Paris. They managed the capitalist industry that was replacing the craft shops and guilds of the past; they welcomed the doctrine . . . that free enterprise would be more stimulating and productive than the traditional regulation of industry and trade by the state. They financed and organized the transformation of raw materials into finished goods, and transported these from producer to consumer, making a profit at both ends. They benefited from thirty thousand miles of the best roads in Europe, but they denounced the obstructive tolls that were charged on the roads and canals of France, and the different weights and measures jealously maintained by individual provinces. They controlled the commerce that was enriching Bordeaux, Marseilles, and Nantes; . . . they widened the market from the town to the world; and through such trade they developed for France an overseas empire second only to England's. They felt that they, not the nobility, were the creators of France's growing wealth, and they determined to share equally with nobles and clergy in governmental favors and appointments, in status before the law and at the royal courts, in access to all the privileges and graces of French society. When Manon Roland [the respected wife of Interior Minister Jean-Marie Roland de La Platière], refined and accomplished but bourgeoise, was invited to visit a titled lady, and was asked to eat with the servants there instead of sitting at table with the noble guests, she raised a cry of protest that went to the hearts of the middle class. Such resentments and aspirations were in their thoughts when they joined in the revolutionary motto,

"Liberty, equality, and fraternity"; they did not mean it downward as well as upward, but it served its purpose until it could be revised. Meanwhile the bourgeoisie became the most powerful of the forces that were making for revolution.

It was they who filled the theaters and applauded [playwright Pierre-Augustin] Beaumarchais' satires of the aristocracy. It was they, even more than the nobility, who joined the Freemason lodges to work for freedom of life and thought; they who read Voltaire and relished his erosive wit, and agreed with [Edward] Gibbon that all religions are equally false for the philosopher and equally useful for the statesman. . . .

THE ROLE OF THE AVERAGE CITIZEN

The "people," in the terminology of the Revolution, meant the peasants and the town workers. Even in the towns the factory employees were a minority of the population; the picture there was not a succession of factories but rather a humming medley of butchers, bakers, brewers, grocers, cooks, peddlers, barbers, shopkeepers, innkeepers, vintners, carpenters, masons, house painters, glass workers, plasterers, tilers, shoemakers, dressmakers, dyers, cleaners, tailors, blacksmiths, servants, cabinetmakers, saddlers, wheelwrights, goldsmiths, cutlers, weavers, tanners, printers, booksellers, prostitutes, and thieves. These workers wore ankle-length pantaloons rather than the knee breeches *(culottes)* and stockings of the upper classes; so they were named "sansculottes," ["without culottes"], and as such they played a dramatic part in the Revolution. The influx of gold and silver from the New World, and the repeated issuance of paper money, raised prices everywhere in Europe; in France, between 1741 and 1789, they rose 65 percent, while wages rose 22 percent. In Lyons 30,000 persons were on relief in 1787; in Paris 100,000 families were listed as indigent in 1791. Labor unions for economic action were forbidden; so were strikes, but they were frequent. As the Revolution neared, the workers were in an increasingly despondent and rebellious mood. Give them guns and a leader, and they would . . . depose the King.

The peasants of France, in 1789, were presumably better off than a century before. . . . They were better off than the other peasants of Continental Europe, possibly excepting those of northern Italy. About a third of the tilled land was held by peasant proprietors; a third was farmed out by noble, ecclesiastical, or bourgeois owners to tenants or sharecroppers; the rest was worked by hired hands under supervision by the owner or his steward. More and more of the owners—themselves harassed by rising costs and keener competition—were enclosing, for tillage or pasturage, "common lands" on which the peasants had formerly been free to graze their cattle or gather wood.

All but a few . . . peasant holders were subject to feudal dues. They were bound by contract charter to give the seigneur—the lord of the manor—several days of unpaid labor every year (the *corvée*) to aid him in farming his land and repairing his roads; and they paid him a toll whenever they used those roads. They owed him a moderate quitrent annually in produce or cash. If they sold their holding he was entitled to 10 or 15 percent of the purchase price. They paid him if they fished in his waters or pastured their animals on his field. They owed him a fee every time they used his mill, his bake-house, his wine- or oil-press. . . .

To support the Church that blessed his crops, formed his children to obedience and belief, and dignified his life with sacraments, the peasant contributed to it annually a tithe—usually less than a tenth—of his produce. Heavier than tithe or feudal dues were the taxes laid upon him by the state: a poll or head tax . . . the . . . twentieth of his yearly income, a sales tax . . . on his every purchase of gold or silver ware, metal products, alcohol, paper, starch . . . , and the *gabelle,* which required him to buy in each year a prescribed amount of salt from the government at a price fixed by the government. As the nobility and the clergy found legal or illegal ways of avoiding many of these taxes . . . the main burden of support for state and Church, in war and peace, fell upon the peasantry.

Burdened by high taxes and faced with famine, the French peasantry rose up in protest against the government in 1789.

These taxes, tithes, and feudal dues could be borne when harvests were good, but they brought misery when, through war damages or the weather's whims, the harvest turned bad, and a year's exhausting toil seemed spent in vain. Then many peasant owners sold their land or their labor, or both, to luckier gamblers with the soil.

STORMS, FLOODS, FAMINE

The year 1788 was marked by merciless "acts of God." A severe drought stunted crops; a hailstorm, raging from Normandy to Champagne, devastated 180 miles of usually fertile terrain; the winter (1788–89) was the severest in eighty years; fruit trees perished by the thousands. The spring of 1789 loosed disastrous floods; the summer brought famine to almost every province. State, church, and private charity strove to get food to the starving; only a few individuals died of hunger, but millions came close to the end of their resources. [The cities of] Caen, Rouen, Orléans, Nancy, Lyons, saw rival groups fighting like animals for corn; Marseilles saw 8,000 famished people at its gates threatening to invade and pillage the city; in Paris the working-class district of St.-Antoine had 30,000 paupers to be cared for. Meanwhile a trade-easing treaty with Great Britain (1786) had deluged France with industrial products down-pricing native goods and throwing thousands of French laborers out of work—25,000 in Lyons, 46,000 in Amiens, 80,000 in Paris. In March 1789, peasants refused to pay taxes, adding to fears of national bankruptcy. . . .

THE KING AND MARIE ANTOINETTE

[King Louis XVI] was a good man, but hardly a good king. He had not expected to rule, but the early death of his father . . . made him, at the age of twenty, master of France. He had no desire to govern men; he had a knack with tools, and was an excellent locksmith. He preferred hunting to ruling; he counted that day lost in which he had not shot a stag; between 1774 and 1789 he ran down 1,274 of them, and killed 189,251 game; yet he was always unwilling to order the death of a man. . . . Returning from his hunts he ate to the steadily increasing capacity of his stomach. He became fat but strong, with the gentle strength of a giant who fears to crush with his embrace. Marie Antoinette judged her husband well: "The King is not a coward; he possesses abundance of passive courage, but he is overwhelmed by an awkward shyness and mistrust of himself. . . . He is afraid to command. . . . He lived like a child, and always ill at ease, under the eyes of [his grandfather King] Louis XV, until the age of twenty-one. This constraint confirmed his timidity."

His love for his Queen was part of his undoing. She was beautiful and stately, she graced his court with her charm and gaiety. . . . [Louis] amused his courtiers, and shamed his ancestors, by being visibly devoted to his wife. He gave her costly jewels, but she and France wanted a child. When children came she proved to be a good mother, suffering with their ailments and moderating nearly all her faults except her pride (she had never been less than part of royalty) and her repeated intervention in affairs of state. Here she had some excuses, for Louis could seldom choose or keep a course, and often waited for the Queen to make up his mind; some courtiers wished he had her quick judgment and readiness to command.

The King did all he could to meet the crises laid upon him by the weather, the famine, the bread riots, the revolt against taxes, the demands of the nobility and the Parlement, the expenses of the court and the administration, and the growing deficit in the Treasury. . . .

After some months of hesitation and chaos, the King called Jacques Necker, a Swiss Protestant financier domiciled in Paris, to be director of the Treasury (1777–81). Under this alien and heretical leadership Louis undertook a brave program of minor reforms. He allowed the formation of elected local and provincial assemblies to serve as the voice of their constituents in bridging the gap between the people and the government. He shocked the nobles by denouncing the *corvée*, and by declaring, in a public statement (1780), "The taxes of the poorest part of our subjects [have] increased, in proportion, much more than all the rest"; and he expressed his "hopes that rich people will not think themselves wronged when they will have to meet the charges which long since they should have shared with others." He freed the last of the serfs on his own lands, but resisted Necker's urging to require a like measure from the nobility and the clergy. He established pawnshops to lend money to the poor at three percent. He forbade the use of torture in the examination of witnesses or criminals. He proposed to abolish the dungeons at [the prison of] Vincennes and to raze the Bastille [prison] as items in a program of prison reform. Despite his piety and orthodoxy he allowed a considerable degree of religious liberty to Protestants and Jews. He refused to punish free thought, and allowed the ruthless pamphleteers of Paris to lampoon him as a cuckold, his wife as a harlot, and his children as bastards. He forbade his government to spy into the private correspondence of the citizens.

With the enthusiastic support of Beaumarchais and the *philosophes*, and over the objections of Necker (who predicted that such a venture would complete the bankruptcy of France), Louis sent material and financial aid, amounting to $240,000,000, to the American colonies in their struggle for independence; it was a French fleet, and the battalions of Lafayette [a French statesman and soldier turned American general] . . . that helped [General George] Washington to bottle up [British general Charles] Cornwallis . . . compelling him to surrender and so bring the war to a close. But democratic ideas swept across the Atlantic into France, the Treasury stumbled under its new debts, Necker was dismissed (1781), and the bourgeois bondholders clamored for financial control of the government.

Meanwhile the Parlement of Paris pressed its claim to check the monarchy through a veto power over the decrees of the King; and Louis-Philippe-Joseph, Duc d'Orléans—his cousin . . . almost openly schemed to capture the throne. Through . . . agents he scattered money and promises among politicians, pamphleteers, orators, and prostitutes. He threw open to his followers the facilities, court, and gardens of his Palais-Royal; cafés, wineshops, bookstores and gambling clubs sprang up to accommodate the crowd that gathered there day and night; . . . pamphlets were born there every hour; speeches resounded from platforms, tables, and chairs; plots were laid for the deposition of the King.

ASKING ADVICE FROM THE PEOPLE

Harassed to desperation, Louis recalled Necker to the Ministry of Finance (1788). On Necker's urging, and as a last and perilous resort that might save or overthrow his throne, he issued, on August 8, 1788, a call to the communities of France to elect and send to Versailles their leading nobles, clerics, and commoners to form (as had last been done in 1614) a [legislature called] States- or Estates-General that would give him advice and support in meeting the problems of the realm.

There were some remarkable features about this historic call to the country by a government that for almost two centuries had apparently thought of the commonalty as merely food providers, taxpayers, and [soldiers]. First the King, again at Necker's urging, and over nobiliar protests, announced that the Third Estate should have as many deputies and votes, in the coming assembly, as the two other estates combined. Second, the election was to be by the nearest approach yet made in France to universal adult suffrage: any male aged twenty-seven or more, who had paid in the past year any state tax however small, was eligible to vote for the local assemblies that would choose the deputies to represent the region in Paris. Third, the King added to his call a request to all electoral assemblies to submit to him *cahiers,* or reports, that would specify the problems and needs of each class in each district, with recommendations for remedies and reforms. Never before, in the memory of Frenchmen, had any of their kings asked advice of his people.

Of the 615 *cahiers* taken to the King by the delegates, 545 survive. Nearly all of them express their loyalty to him, and even their affection for him as clearly a man of goodwill; but nearly all propose that he share his problems and powers with an elected assembly that would make up with him a constitutional monarchy. None mentioned the divine right of kings. All demanded trial by jury, privacy of the mails, moderation of taxes, and reform of the law. The *cahiers* of the nobility stipulated that in the coming States-General each of the orders should sit and vote separately, and no measure should become law unless approved by all three estates. The *cahiers* of the clergy called for an end to religious toleration, and for full and exclusive control of education by the Church. The *cahiers* of the Third Estate reflected, with diverse emphasis, the demands of the peasants for a reduction of taxes, abolition of serfdom and feudal dues, universalization of free education, the protection of farms from injury by the hunts and animals of the seigneurs; and the hopes of the middle class for careers open to talent regardless of birth, for an end to transport tolls, for the extension of taxes to the nobility and the clergy; some proposed that the King should wipe out the fiscal deficit by confiscating and selling ecclesiastical property. The first stages of the Revolution were already outlined in these *cahiers.*

In this humble call of a king to his citizens there was a noticeable deviation from impartiality. Whereas outside Paris any man who had paid a tax was eligible to vote, in Paris only those could vote who had paid a poll tax of six livres or more. Perhaps the King and his advisers hesitated to leave to the 500,000 sansculottes the selection of men to represent in the States-General the best intelligence of the capital; the democratic problem of quality versus quantity, of getting brains by counting noses, appeared here on the eve of the Revolution that was, in 1793, to declare for democracy. So the sansculottes were left out of the legitimate drama, and were led to feel that only through the violent force of their number could they express their . . . general will. They would be heard from, they would be avenged. In 1789 they would take the Bastille; in 1792 they would dethrone the King; in 1793 they would be the government of France.

POPULATION GROWTH AND HUMAN SURVIVAL

JOHN ROBERTS

One of the primary causes of social unrest in Europe at the end of the eighteenth century was the rapidly expanding birth rate. English economist Thomas Robert Malthus was one of the first scholars to express alarm over this population explosion, and in 1798 he anonymously published *An Essay on the Principle of Population as It Affects the Future Improvement of Society*. As historian John Roberts explains, Malthus stated that the lives of the poor could never improve because the earth could not support the needs of so many people. By the mid-nineteenth century, the Malthusian theory on population growth was a well-accepted fact by those who promoted birth control, which was illegal in most countries. The words of Malthus continue to be quoted today by environmentalists and others who seek to reduce the human impact on the earth.

[I n] the middle of the eighteenth century Europe's population [began] to grow at an increasing rate, so that by 1850 it was nearly double what it had been a century before, and stood at about 260 millions. This represented an increased proportion of the total world population, of which Europe now contained something over one-fifth and nowhere else except in the new United States did population grow so fast. . . .

This overall picture cloaks important differences between countries. Spain had more inhabitants than Great Britain in 1800,

Excerpted from *Revolution and Improvement: The Western World, 1775–1847*, by John Roberts. Copyright © 1976 John Roberts. Reprinted by permission of the University of California Press.

but was left behind by her fifty years later. In Europe, British population grew fastest of all. In the century after 1750 it increased by seventy per cent, while that of Russia grew forty-two per cent and France twenty-six per cent. Clearly, there were important social and political implications in these figures. Some countries still grew very slowly long after 1800.

Nevertheless, the fact of overall growth soon provoked notice and an important change of attitude. Almost everywhere except in the United States, demographic change seemed to reveal new problems for rulers and economists, changed existing relationships and through them attitudes and ideas. . . . A more alarming idea had been put forward in a book of 1790 by a Venetian writer, Ortès, who noted that population grew by geometrical progression, while the possibilities of producing food were finite. This idea was given a far wider audience in an anonymous book published in England in 1798, which was to be one of the most influential works of the century. This was the *Essay on Population*, as it was soon shortly termed, of the Reverend Thomas Malthus.

UNDERFED WRETCHES

Malthus's work was published at the beginning of one of the greatest creative surges of English culture and in a society already assuming the economic leadership of the world. Thus sufficiently explains its success when taken into account against the all too visible background of population growth. France was full of beggars in 1789. English villages swarmed with underfed wretches for whom there seemed to be not enough work to go round and whose plight was already leading to attacks on the system of English poor relief. Malthus attempted an overall explanation of the great paradox that a society which seemed to grow richer and richer might contain huge numbers in miserable poverty.

His argument was brutally simple and may be condensed in a few of his sentences:

> The power of population is indefinitely greater than the power of the earth to produce subsistence for man. . . . Population, when unchecked, increases in a geometrical ratio. Subsistence only increases in an arithmetical ratio. . . . There are few states in which there is not a constant effort in the population to increase beyond the means of subsistence. This constant effort as constantly tends to subject the lower class of society to distress, and to prevent any great permanent melioration [improvement] of their condition.

This message was instantly and continuously compelling in spite of Malthus's drab style. He revealed—or appeared to reveal—

that growth was not a beneficent harbinger of plenty, as had been thought, but the spectre of coming disasters.

Malthus based his assumptions about the different rates at which population and subsistence would grow on what he believed to be the fact that human sexuality (and therefore the tendency to reproduce) was a constant pressure and that, however large it might be, there was a limit to the amount of land which might grow food. . . . Malthus quickly became famous—or notorious—for his exposition of the laws which, he said, normally held population in check. Foremost among them were the positive checks of famine and disease. If they ceased or were not to operate, said Malthus, then only a "preventive" check could prevent population growing to a size at which it would outrun food supply. At that point, it would initiate again the positive checks of famine and disease. By a preventive check he meant one which would not permit growth to the point at which the positive ones would operate. He summed this up as "moral restraint," a prescription, in effect, that people should marry later; he would countenance neither abortion nor contraception (though, ironically, nineteenth-century advocates of the latter were to be called "neo-Malthusians").

INESCAPABLE LAWS OF NATURE

These ideas had enormous effect. His German translator called Malthus another [Isaac] Newton. Specifically, their impact was greatest on economics, but it was in 1838 that a naturalist, Charles Darwin, suddenly found in reading Malthus a key to the evolutionary process in the competition for survival. More generally, it gave a damaging blow to the optimistic belief in potentially limitless progress of so much advanced thought of the eighteenth century. This had been Malthus's purpose and his book's full title showed it: *An Essay on the Principle of Population as It Affects the Future Improvement of Society.* He wished to demonstrate that between Man and his perfectibility as a species lay inescapable laws of nature, whose operation, if ignored, must ensure even greater misery than if their existence were recognized. In practice, this seemed to mean that misery for some was inescapable, that the poor would always be with you, and that they ought to minimize their sufferings by cultivating prudence in the avoidance of early marriage. There can be little doubt, unfortunately, that for all Malthus's own mildness of disposition and disinterested benevolence, this was to become a powerful deterrent to political reform, for it suggested that all attempts to remove misery and poverty by institutional change were in vain.

WORLD HISTORY BY ERA

1800–1812

CHAPTER 3

Haiti Declares Independence from France

Selden Rodman

When Christopher Columbus sailed to the New World in 1492, the first place he landed was an island he named Hispaniola. In the late eighteenth century the island was colonized by the French and renamed Saint-Domingue. By using more than half a million African slaves to produce sugar, Saint-Domingue provided vast wealth to the French treasury back in Paris. To maintain control of the island, white administrators employed light-skinned blacks of mixed blood—known as mulattos (*gens de couleur* in French)—to oversee the slaves.

In 1789, inspired by the French Revolution, the slaves in the colony staged a long and bloody war to throw off the chains of European oppression. As Selden Rodman, a poet, anthropologist, and frequent visitor to Haiti, writes, the rebellion was led by a former slave named Toussaint-Louverture. The blacks vanquished the whites and mulattos and gained control of the colony. But in 1802 Emperor Napoléon I sent tens of thousands of soldiers to take back the island for France. Napoléon's troops failed miserably, however, and in 1804 independence was declared, the island was renamed Haiti, and the first black republic in the Western Hemisphere was founded.

[T he northern side of Saint-Domingue] boasted a thousand plantation houses behind monumental pillared gateways. It sparkled at night with the gay illumination of elaborate balls, lighted carriages, and the glaring ovens and stacks of boiling-houses refining sugarcane 'round the clock. At its western extremity Cap Français (now Cap Haïtien), a city of 25,000 with fine public buildings and theatres of stone and brick, was properly known as "The Paris of the Antilles." In prosperous years as many as 80,000 seamen and 700 ships were employed to move [the island's] products to [France] the Mother Country. . . .

To the south, connected by splendid roads, Port-au-Prince, a town of 8,000, was beginning to assert itself as the outlet for a naturally dry region brought under cultivation by artificial irrigation. As the capital of the southernmost province, Les Cayes, with its own small but very fertile plain, was flourishing, but on the whole the South Peninsula remained undeveloped. . . .

WHITES, BLACKS, AND PEOPLE OF COLOR

Who was responsible for this immense productivity, a wealth so suddenly come by that its brash spenders were regarded with envious dislike by even the gilded courtiers at [French king] Louis XV's [palace at] Versailles?

The 36,000 Whites who administered the affairs of Saint-Domingue up until 1791 were not only convinced that it was their work alone. They regarded [the government in] Paris . . . with its social snobbism, its increasing import duties, and its codes of fair treatment for (colonial) labor, with contemptuous distrust. That they should regard the Paris of [revolutionaries such as] Mirabeau, Marat and Robespierre with more than merely distrust was inevitable.

Next in line of privilege, 28,000 *gens de couleur* [people of color or mixed-blood mulattoes] comprised all free persons who had African blood in their veins. These [mulattoes] who by 1791 owned almost one-third of the land, including the better part of the fertile parish of Jérémie, owed their existence to [a 1685 royal decree] which had stated that a slave acquiring freedom either by gift or purchase was to become a full French citizen, with all rights, even including the ownership of slaves of his own. . . . The Mulattoes, living in constant fear of the mass of Negro slaves— at least of falling back into their wholly unprivileged ranks— were in turn held in check by the . . . politically dominant and socially secure ruling caste of "pure" Whites; and the means of doing so consisted of imposition of the most humiliating and cruelly enforced racial legislation ever up to that time conceived by man. [Historian James] Leyburn . . . listed . . . the steps by which the white planters discriminated against the Mulattoes:

> . . . He might not fill any responsible office either in the courts or the militia, for that would elevate him above

white persons. Certain careers, such as goldsmithing, were closed to him because they brought wealth; others, notably medicine and the apothecary's art, were forbidden on the ground that whites might be poisoned; law and religion were barred to him because of their public and honorific nature. Colored women were forbidden in 1768 to marry white men. In 1779 began a series of laws designed to humiliate the colored person in public: his clothes must be of a different material and cut from the white person's; he must be indoors by nine o'clock in the evening; he might not sit in the same section of churches and theatres with whites.

BRUTALITY AGAINST SLAVES

Unlike the Whites and the Mulattoes, the 500,000 Negro slaves could not claim title to the unparalleled wealth of Saint-Domingue; they were too busy producing it. In addition, of course, they were illiterate, without spokesmen or recognized means of protest—without privileges of any kind. So relentless, indeed, was the pace at which the slaves were driven to work, that it is estimated their entire number had to be replaced every twenty years. The inexhaustible source of supply, of course, was Africa. Chained neck-to-neck in the pestilential holds of slave-ships, only the very strongest survived even the hazards of the "Middle Passage."

Dahomeans, Nagos, Congos, Aradas, Fans, Ibos, Mandingues, Capalaous and members of a hundred other proud tribes from the West Coast [of Africa] were driven to work in Saint-Domingue with whips and if they showed a disposition to protest were flogged to death, buried alive, thrown into ovens or horribly mutilated. . . .

Two things alone sustained the slaves in this seemingly hopeless ordeal: their hatred of the master race and their participation in the religious ceremonials of their ancestors. Both consolations, of course, had to be indulged in secret. Slaves who could escaped into the mountain fastnesses; known as *marrons,* they descended upon the more isolated plantations from time to time. . . . But the religious rites [voodoo] sometimes disguised as innocent "dances" and therefore tolerated by the planters as a kind of "safety valve," provided the real means of subversive organization and of contact between the *marrons* and their unliberated comrades.

THE INSURRECTION

The spark that was to ignite this magazine of suppressed fury was the French Revolution. When word came in 1789 that delegates were to be nominated to the [governing body] States-General after a lapse of 150 years, the planters made two strategic blunders. They sent no fewer than 37 delegates to Paris to air their "grievances," and they asserted by implication that the only solution to their problems was complete freedom to determine their own course regardless of Paris. The answer of the National Assembly came quickly. A resolution was passed granting political rights to the *gens de couleur*. Two young leaders of the Mulattoes, Ogé and Chavannes, observing that the Whites had no intention of obeying this directive, organized a demonstration at Cap Français to which the colonial police replied in March of 1791 by seizing them and breaking them on the wheel in public.

It was at this juncture, when the Mulattoes were beginning to see that their rights were not to be gained except by force, that the unexpected happened. The 500,000 Negro slaves revolted. Their insurrection was plotted at a [voodoo] ceremony in the Plaine presided over by a *papaloi* (priest) named Boukman. Six days later, on August 20, the slaves set fire to the plantation houses and drove those masters they could not lay their hands on into the fortified towns. The Mulattoes, with no alternative, tried at first to make friends with the leaders of the Blacks and turn the insurrection to their advantage.

In the two years of confused struggle that followed, the French, with revolutions and foreign wars of their own to contend with at home, attempted to keep the disastrous situation in their richest possession in hand by sending Commissioners with instructions to appease the three warring factions. But when one of them, an unscrupulous Jacobin named Sonthonax, exceeded his orders by decreeing the immediate freedom of the slaves and giving them the keys to Cap Français, Rigaud, the able leader of the Mulattoes who had played a major part in expelling the British from the undefended Southwest, broke with the Negroes.

A Leader Emerges from Chaos

At this critical moment there came to the front of the stage the ablest figure in Haitian history. . . . Nearly fifty years old at the time of the 1791 revolt, in which he took no part except to assist the family of his master to escape, Toussaint Louverture had early in his life been recognized for his intelligence, taught to read French, and elevated from stable-boy (in which capacity he may have learned the superb horsemanship he later exhibited) to coachman. He was a small man and very homely, but shrewd and fearless and capable of inspiring a fanatical devotion among his followers. . . .

When war broke out between France and Spain in 1793, Toussaint had joined the Spanish with six-hundred disciplined [black soldiers] and induced a number of French regular troops who had deserted to train and officer his ragged but growing army. By the spring of 1794 he was in command of 4,000 men. That summer, when the English were threatening to take advantage of the French debacle by appearing as champions of the Whites and Mulattoes, Toussaint without warning deserted Spain and arrived in Cap Français as the saviour of Sonthonax and his nominal superior, the French Governor-General Laveaux. In a series of brilliant campaigns Toussaint and Rigaud succeeded in all but eliminating the British. . . .

Sonthonax, meanwhile, who had had no difficulty in outwitting Negro leaders in the past, made the fatal mistake of trying to increase his own power by backing Toussaint and getting Laveaux recalled to France. Laveaux departed, but Toussaint promptly had the surprised Commissioner "elected" deputy to France, and, backed by several thousand troops, politely escorted him to shipboard. . . .

1801 was Toussaint's year of full power . . . and his last year on the stage of history. It began with the capture of Santo Domingo, the Spanish capital in the East, and the subjection of the entire island to Black rule. Ten years of revolution had left Haiti in ruins. The towns were destroyed, the fields were no longer cultivated, the great irrigation works in the Artibonite and Cul-de-Sac plains were destroyed beyond repair. In that year, partly by appealing to the pride of the Negroes, partly by using his armies to enforce discipline on the plantations, and partly by negotiating favorable trade agreements with France's enemies, England and the United States, Toussaint managed to restore most of the prosperity of the old Colony. This ex-slave who had once assisted his white master to escape from Boukman's incendiaries now welcomed back the former planters as administrators; respected contracts; and sought to heal the terrible wounds inflicted by racial warfare. . . . The Constitution of May 9, 1801, was drawn up by a committee consisting of seven Whites and three Mulattoes. Toussaint neglected nothing to convince a hostile world that the first Negro state was prosperous, law-abiding and enlightened. But it was not to be.

NAPOLEON STRIKES BACK

In fact it was inevitable that Napoleon, whose star had risen in the meanwhile, should look with irritation upon this growing menace to his colonial ambitions. This "gilded African," as he called Toussaint, had re-awakened dreams of the fabulous lost treasure of Saint-Domingue—and there he stood athwart the road to empire in North America! All during the year 1801 the shipyards of [the French cities of] Brest and Marseilles rang with preparations for the largest combined operation and transoceanic expeditionary force in history. The dictator's private orders to the commander of this force of 20,000 veterans of Campo Formio and Arcola, his brother-in-law [Charles-Victor-Emmanuel] Leclerc, were succinct: in the first fortnight the coastal towns were to be taken; that accomplished, a converging movement would smash resistence in the interior; in the third phase, flying columns would hunt down the remaining resistors. . . .

On February 5, 1802, Leclerc, with a detachment of 5,000 men, went ashore off Cap Français. Christophe, the Negro commander whom Toussaint had placed in charge of the capital of the North, followed his instructions far enough to fire the city and retire to the hills. By February 6 Leclerc controlled the Plaine du Nord. The same day Port-au-Prince fell to another detachment, its principal fort which Toussaint had entrusted to a Mulatto surrendering to the French with shouts of "Vive la France!" Another Mulatto officer, Laplume, voluntarily surrendered the South Province. Only [two commanders] offered resistance as they retreated inland. . . . On February 23 Toussaint's strong point in the Ravine de Couleuvres was stormed and the French drove on into Gonaïves, but Toussaint, thanks to [his commander Jean-Jacques] Dessalines' support of his left flank, was permitted to escape with the bulk of his army and retire into the eastern Artibonite Valley. It remained for Leclerc to dispose of this concentration.

The decisive battle took place at the entrance to the valley the final week of March. Crête-a-Pierrot, an almost impregnable position, was garrisoned with a picked regiment of 1,200 Negroes commanded by Dessalines. Leclerc took it at a cost of 2,000 men, allowing half the garrison to cut its way to freedom. But the Black resistance was broken. Christophe went over to the French, and exposed by this defection, Toussaint and Dessalines capitulated on the promise of generous terms May 1.

Toussaint and Leclerc had each made a major mistake. Toussaint had put too much trust in his trained army of 20,000, and its officers, many of whom were motivated more by envy of his brilliance and hatred of the Blacks than by hostility to Leclerc; if he had armed the 400,000 remaining ex-slaves and instructed them in guerrilla warfare the French general's position would have been hopeless from the outset. Leclerc's mistake, if it can be called one, was in being unable to disguise Napoleon's real intention: the re-imposition of . . . slavery on Saint-Domingue. The news that people had already been re-enslaved on [the island of] Guadaloupe leaked out, and this, confirmed by the seizure of Toussaint, made it impossible for Leclerc to dissolve popular resistance before the advent of his ultimate and fatal adversary: Yellow Fever.

FINAL VICTORY

Already weakened by the loss of half his effectives in battle—to the point where he was in no position to risk guerrilla warfare by dealing with Christophe and Dessalines as he had with Toussaint—Leclerc encountered, June 1, his first case of the terrible disease. By the end of the month 4,000 officers and men were dead. Leclerc himself was fighting off bouts of malaria when the news spread over the island that the French—contrary to his promises—had officially restored slavery in *all* their colonies. At once the fanatical North was up in arms. The Black generals slipped away and made peace with the Mulattoes, now regrouping in a South under the leadership of [Alexandre] Pétion. Through July and August with his reinforcements dropping dead almost as soon as they landed, Leclerc wrote letters of desperation to Paris. The fear that Toussaint might escape from France and return to head up the rebellion became an obsession. On November 2, while writing a last frantic appeal to Napoleon for more troops, Leclerc himself succumbed to Yellow Fever.

[Jean-Baptiste-Donatien de Vimeur, comte de] Rochambeau, the new Governor-General, took over, and in his desperation went so far as to import from Jamaica 1,500 bloodhounds at over $100 apiece to track down the Blacks and disembowel them, but it was too late. The resumption of war with England on May 12 cut Rochambeau's lines of communications. Defeated by Dessalines and [fellow commander] Capoix-la-Morte at Vertières outside Le Cap on November 18, 1803, the French general surrendered his sword to the waiting English admiral on his flagship. The French, who had spent millions and sacrificed 50,000 men to recapture Saint-Domingue, were gone never to return. And Napoleon's ambition of making Hispaniola a stepping stone to Louisiana and the ultimate conquest of the New World came to nothing.

On January 1, 1804, at Gonaïves, Dessalines proclaimed the independence of the colony, re-naming it "Haiti," and settled down to the task of restoring order and prosperity in a land devastated by thirteen years of unremitting combat. But his first act in the presence of the victorious army was symbolically fateful. Seizing the tricolor of France from its standard he tore out the white section and announced that henceforth the new nation's flag would be red and black alone.

THE LUDDITES SMASH FACTORIES

BRIAN BAILEY

In the early nineteenth century the Industrial Revolution created widespread unemployment among textile workers, who were replaced by machines. Coupled with food shortages and economic hardships caused by Great Britain's ongoing war with France, a violent revolt among the working class ensued.

The unemployed workers, calling themselves Luddites, after a legendary boy named Ludham who broke his father's knitting loom, smashed textile machinery, vandalized factories, and initiated a class war whose intensity had rarely been seen in England.

The Luddite movement began in the hosiery and lace industries around 1811 and spread to the wool and cotton mills over the next several years. Those who participated in the industrial sabotage were treated harshly by the government—more than a dozen were hanged in York alone in 1813. Although the movement soon collapsed, the term Luddite continues to be used for people who are perceived as opposing progress.

Brian Bailey, a full-time author who has written more than twenty books, describes the harsh conditions in England that led to the Luddite rebellion.

The later years of the reign of George III encompassed a period of stark contrasts in British society. The prosperous and imaginative surface appearance of the country obscured a host of social evils, like a made-up face and upholstered body disguising the true features of an ageing prostitute. The nation was poised on the threshold of new standards of triumph and civilisation. The third quarter of the eighteenth century saw the inventions of [James] Hargreaves' spinning jenny, [Richard] Arkwright's spinning frame and [Samuel] Crompton's [muslin wheel]. James Watt built his first steam engine, and the pioneering Bridgewater Canal was constructed between Worsley and Manchester to carry coal to industry. [Edmund] Cartwright's power-loom was on the horizon. Mass-production machinery, powered by water or steam, was soon inducing capitalist manufacturers to build huge mills of brick in Lancashire and of stone across the Pennines [region]. Alongside the rise of the cotton industry in Lancashire, . . . Yorkshire was becoming dominant in the woollen industry, succeeding the smaller early mills in rural parts of England. . . . Silk manufacturing was becoming important to Cheshire and Derbyshire, and the latter county has the distinction of hosting the first factory in the modern sense, with many employees going out to work in one building at machinery operated, in this case, by water power. . . .

The rise of manufacturing industries and the beginning of the railway revolution were accompanied by the abolition of slavery and reforms of prison and factory conditions. . . . It was the [literary] age of [Lord George] Byron and [William] Wordsworth, Jane Austen and Sir Walter Scott. . . . But there was a reverse side to this fashionable . . . facade . . . [and it was] the development of an economic and social climate in the textile industries of the Midlands and north of England that made them ripe for unrest and the advent of Luddism.

The revolution in industry was about to cause the biggest destabilisation of British civilisation since the Black Death in the fourteenth century. Since that time, once . . . some social stability [had been] restored, economic development had progressed at a pace which the working population of the country could cope with. But the rapid changes in technology which began three centuries later were responsible for huge upheavals throughout working-class society. A mass movement of workers from rural to urban centres was accompanied by vast population increases: in the course of the eighteenth century the population of England almost doubled. The new manufacturing towns soon became overcrowded, with the inevitable consequences of slums, widespread disease and rising crime rates. . . . The majority of them were crimes against property—the obsession of Georgian criminal law.

LAWS AGAINST UNIONS

Dealing with the large increase in crime was one of the chief preoccupations of local authorities. But these authorities were made up largely of land-owning country squires, while law and order lay in the hands of parish constables. The latter were becoming as unequal to their hugely mounting task as the squires were to bringing about urgently needed social reforms. The wealthy and powerful believed there was a "criminal class" which must be eliminated for the sake of society as a whole, and acted upon this delusion with a barbarity almost unparalleled in the peacetime history of Europe. In 1801 a boy of thirteen was hanged for stealing a spoon. . . .

Such hysterical fear and suspicion of the "lower orders" found expression in political terms, too, in the measures taken . . . against what it perceived as a [revolutionary] tendency among the working populace. . . . In 1799 the Corresponding Societies Act suppressed the circulation of radical literature by bodies such as the London Corresponding Society, which had been founded after the publication of Thomas Paine's *The Rights of Man,* with a membership composed chiefly of artisans and tradesmen. . . . And in 1799 and 1800 repressive Combination Acts reinforced existing laws against trade unions, making it a criminal offence for workers to join forces in pressing their employers for higher wages or the reduction of working hours; or indeed, to gather together for any industrial or political purpose whatever. . . .

The Combination laws were passed . . . in an atmosphere of near panic. The rise of working-class radicalism in England at the same time as revolution in France and the apparent inability of the primitive policing system to maintain law and order in rapidly expanding industrial towns had already led to several repressive measures. The Combination Acts served a dual purpose. Not only did they render workmen who combined to protect their wages and conditions liable to prosecution for conspiracy— a capital felony—they also eliminated one of the cradles of subversive intercourse. But there could be no moral justification for leaving workers at the mercy of unscrupulous employers, without, in the first place, any right to protect themselves by joining trade unions which could represent their interests fairly and legally, and, in the second place, without any regulation of their wages and working conditions. The government's policy of nonintervention in industrial disputes was called *laissez-faire.* It had become . . . the political dogma of the English bourgeoisie. In fact, it represented freedom for the employers and intolerable repression of the workers. Individual freedom after the Combination Acts meant the freedom of capitalist employers to exploit their workers in any way they chose. But drive men into a corner, and their only defence is attack.

The effectiveness of the legislation varied from trade to trade.

Unions were often merely driven underground, or survived in the guise of friendly societies. Many illegal unions continued to exist, in one way or another, in the textile industries. In theory, the law prevented manufacturers, as well as workers, from combining in a common interest, but this reminds one rather of [the sarcastic] comment on the "impartiality of the law which forbids rich and poor alike to sleep in doorways." Besides, a workman breaking the law could be sentenced to two months of hard labour, whereas a convicted master was liable only to a fine of £20. . . .

Other factors in the early years of the nineteenth century combined to make the living standards of the working population even more hazardous. The summers of 1809–12 saw disastrous harvests in Britain, but the [war with Napoléon's France] (not to mention poor harvests on the continent as well) precluded the importation of wheat, thus producing a huge increase in the price of bread and other foods. . . .

LUDDITE REBELLION

[These conditions gave rise to] textile machinery saboteurs who became known as Luddites, between 1811 and 1816. . . . The upheavals in working-class life and economy during the Industrial Revolution and the Napoleonic Wars were felt throughout the country and in other trades at the same time. The Luddites, who often had the sympathy and sometimes the bodily reinforcement of other, non-textile workers and tradesmen, were simply organised exponents of physical resistance to worsening conditions. The introduction of the spinning jenny and the gig-mill to the Cotswold wool towns had already caused much hardship to spinners and shearmen in an area threatened by the growing monopoly of Yorkshire in the woollen industry. [Writer] Arthur Young noted that there were "many begging children" in Chippenham in 1796. Stroud and other places had fallen into decay and "almost wholly into beggary," while at Seend, "the poor, from the great reduction in the price of spinning, scarcely have the heart to earn the little that is obtained by it."

The net result of so much inequality and repression in an ill-prepared new industrial society was the development of a class war. The decade preceding the Luddite outbreaks was characterised by rising food prices while trade depression was causing falling wages. In the north the growth of factory industry was having a huge impact on the lives of working people. Domestic textile occupations were being slowly destroyed, and as large manufacturing towns grew rapidly at the expense of the rural economy, capitalist manufacturers were discovering that women and children could be employed to operate factory machinery, and they cost a good deal less in annual wage bills than men.

The inevitable reaction of hard-pressed working men, unable to feed their families and denied the recourse of peaceful collective bargaining to settle their grievances, was to riot and resort to violence.

BEETHOVEN'S REVOLUTIONARY MUSIC

CONRAD L. DONAKOWSKI

Although Ludwig van Beethoven is remembered today as one of the world's greatest musical composers, he was considered a controversial musical revolutionary while alive. As Conrad L. Donakowski, a humanities professor at Michigan State University, explains, Beethoven's romantic works express humanistic views that emphasized the personal worth of the individual and the central importance of human values over religious beliefs.

O n the deepest level . . . the revolutionary [movement] helped to create the idea of the artist as a hero who, relying solely on his own ability, rejects the established system to create his own better one. . . . Because every political system is in some way repressive, it was inevitable that the pure revolutionary zeal of the angry man young at heart became attributable ultimately only to the nonpolitical artist. The genius of the Revolution went underground and emerged in, for one, Beethoven, [an enthusiastic supporter] in the cause of freedom.

After the Revolution, composers were eager to set texts which they could interpret for the people. The humanism of Beethoven's *Ninth* . . . [reminds] us of revolutionary fêtes. . . .

PAINTER IN MUSIC

Yet for the artist the revolutionary era created as many problems as it solved. "If the Revolution in ideas meant the natural goodness of man, the Revolution in fact meant the supremacy of an ill-educated middle class." Though the musician now had fewer ecclesiastical or aristocratic patrons, neither did he seem to fit bourgeois values. . . . In short, no sooner had the artist found himself liberated from [the patronage of] a noble . . . than he found himself again in bondage, this time to bourgeois taste. Hence the discomfiture of serious musicians with both the . . . ossifying churches and the hacks in their own profession, who pandered to crowds interested only in the tenor's high C. Thinking himself a prophet, the romantic artist set out to save the masses from themselves while preserving their folk culture. . . .

In the romantic view, the artist is the aesthetic educator of the people. He rises from the people, or at any rate loves them, and uses their folk expressions as his raw material. . . . To a musician building a new work to express the feelings of humanity gathered in a public festival, monumental styles will seem more attractive than the bald statement of some local song or hymn, although these might provide the raw material for his expression in depth.

Beethoven's life and work were the epitome of this new thinking. His biographers thought that he was the composer who succeeded best in combining high art with something the average man could understand. Some said he was, therefore, the "best painter in music.". . . We know from Beethoven's writings that, if he had a creed, it was that his music was no mere meaningless addition to reality, but an effort to "make explicit, through the medium of his art, the state of consciousness evoked by his profoundest experiences. . . .

The Ninth Symphony transcended the propagandistic chauvinism of the Revolutionary fêtes while depending upon the ideals of liberty, fraternity, and mass-oriented equality for its style. In other hands, the Christian and humanistic legacies were often sordidly manipulated. Napoleon prostituted revolutionary fervor to feed his personal glory. . . . From the romantic viewpoint, a great artist might employ the many honorable ideals which had sprung from civilization without degrading them. The personal ideals of the romantics' favorite rebel, creator and hero, Beetho-

Ludwig van Beethoven

ven, are not simple to define. That he was a humanist of the eighteenth century who proclaimed his. . . independence in his life and music is common knowledge. That he believed music to be an exact though unliteral manifestation of the truth is also evident. That he became a humble man believing in the redemptive value of suffering is equally clear from his writings and music. . . .

The music of Beethoven's two great choral monuments, the *Ninth* and the *Missa Solemnis,* is not a statement of this or that proposition but an expression of the state of soul that can be aroused by those beliefs—the one text humanistic, the other religious. For Beethoven there was no difference. His biographers say that, ideally, the audience should join in singing the last movement of the *Ninth,* that the Gloria of his *Missa Solemnis* is an acclamation by the whole congregation, and that the Finale of the *Ninth* should be a shout. . . . Beethoven wanted to appeal to the multitude, "for he felt the need to communicate his ideas to the masses and to make music a factor in the cultural life of humanity." He wrote that his primary intention in writing the *Missa Solemnis* was to express religious sentiment and impart it to the hearers. . . .

Ecclesiastical rejection of a Beethovenian vocation for music presaged resigned contemplation of an antiworldly goal and rejection of faith in human possibility. Though Beethoven's first Mass had shown a naïve acceptance of ecclesiastical dogma, the second, the *Solemnis,* showed a more critical interpretation. . . . To perform or appreciate the latter demands a wider outlook than mere adherence to the tenets of a certain sect or church. . . . As Joseph d'Ortigue, a pious but understanding critic, was to put it, "Those who see only a musician in Beethoven are badly mistaken: the musician is pedestal for the poet, and I might add for the philosopher." Nevertheless, liturgists and theologians began to say of all artists what one of their number said of Beethoven: "There is nothing religious about him. In vain would one seek an attitude of prayer in his two Masses." A more plausible criticism would have been [fourteenth-century composer Richard] Wagner's statement that one must consider Beethoven's work in historical perspective and realize that the composer was naïvely trying to reform society.

THE POWERFUL PAINTINGS OF GOYA

SYLVIA L. HORWITZ

Francisco José de Goya y Lucientes, born in 1746, was one of the most well-known painters in Spain, and his incredible contrasts of color, light, and shadow have fascinated art lovers throughout the centuries.

In 1786 Goya was appointed court painter to Charles III. Unlike other painters of the time, however, Goya did not idealize his royal subjects and upper-class patrons. When he painted the king's wife, Maria Luisa, for instance, he portrayed her as the remarkably homely, coarse, and corrupt woman he perceived her to be. Goya's other subjects included Spanish underworld characters, madmen in an asylum, and other topics largely ignored by polite society.

As biographer Sylvia L. Horwitz explains, Goya's most horrifying and powerful paintings were inspired by the French invasion of Spain by forces commanded by Emperor Napoléon Bonaparte.

O n March 24, 1808, over streets bright with the capes and flowers strewn by his delirious subjects, Ferdinand VII entered [Madrid] in triumph [and became the new king of Spain]. Unfortunately for the new king, however, Napoleon's troops had beaten him to Madrid by a day.

For several months the French had been penetrating into Spain and occupying its northern strongholds, but [former king] Charles IV had assured his people only a few days before his abdication that "the army of my dear ally, Emperor of the French, traverses my kingdom with ideas of peace and friendship." Napoleon, the nation was told, was there as a partner, merely passing through on his way south to invade Portugal. Many Spaniards even welcomed the French presence as an instrument for reform. But nobody had expected a French column, headed by Joachim Murat, one of Napoleon's most famous marshals, to march into Madrid. An army in transit was one thing; French soldiers in the [main plaza] were another.

NAPOLEON TAKES CONTROL

Like most of his liberal friends, Goya was torn by conflicting emotions. No thinking person could deny the need for changes in Spain, the lack of intellectual freedom, the unconcern for the poor. Yet however much he hungered as a Spanish citizen for social progress, the Spanish patriot within him balked at foreign uniforms. Added to his conflicts of conscience was the burden of age. The First Painter to the Royal Chamber would soon be sixty-two years old.

Four days after Ferdinand VII entered Madrid, on March 28, the San Fernando Academy asked Goya to paint a portrait of him for the conference room. On April 6 and again the day after, the new king sat briefly for his portrait. On April 10 Ferdinand set out from Madrid for France. He had been summarily invited by Napoleon—together with his parents . . . —to a "meeting" in Bayonne, a seaport some thirty miles north, on the coast of France. It was a trap. The Emperor of France had decided to rid both himself and Spain of Bourbons [the ruling family].

Napoleon made short work of Charles IV. He sent the simple-minded ex-king, along with his wife and her lover, still shaken from his recent ordeal, into exile. Ferdinand VII, in his turn, became a comfortably housed prisoner in a French château at Valençay, there to sit out events. Six terrible years of war would pass before Ferdinand again set foot in his capital. Meanwhile—something Napoleon had not counted on—the vengeful, scheming, ruthless young king, who would eventually show his true colors, became in captivity a symbol of national sovereignty. Luridly false stories of his "shameful treatment" at Valençay filtered back to Madrid, turning him into a martyr. In the patriotic thoughts and prayers of his subjects he was fervently referred to as Ferdinand the Desired.

With the old king in exile, the new king a captive, and foreign troops in Madrid, Spain was in upheaval. It took only a rumor, quickly confirmed, to light the fuse of revolt. The news spread from alleyway to alleyway that Napoleon had ordered the remaining members of the royal family to join him in Bayonne. A tradition-bound people foresaw the end of Spanish monarchy, to which they clung doggedly no matter how degenerate it was.

On May 2, 1808, the unarmed citizens of the capital hurled themselves in fury against the French army. With their knives, fists, and stones, *Madrileños* [Madrid citizens] challenged gleaming swords and bayonets. Men wearing thin-soled espadrilles fought booted Imperial Guards. The wrath of the mob reached its peak against Murat's Mamelukes—those turbaned mercenaries from Egypt, formerly slaves, whose very sight evoked ancient memories of the hated Moor.

What Goya saw on the Second of May, either with his own eyes or through those of his friends, he never forgot. Six years later, in 1814, he portrayed *The Charge of the Mamelukes* so vividly that the panic-stricken neighing of horses and the screams of the dying were almost audible. A wild tangle of hooves and manes, of heads and bodies, filled the center of his canvas. Arms were raised in the act of stabbing, curved sabers slashed the air in an atmosphere of frenzy. He splashed violent color over his canvas and used his brush as though it were a weapon in the battle, outlining the massed density of men and horses with thick, heavy, furious strokes.

The fighting raged throughout that unforgettable May Second. It was an unequal battle between citizenry and mercenaries, and ended the day after in savage reprisal and massacre. Murat's troops lost no time in taking revenge on the population. From dawn to dark the streets of Madrid echoed to the sound of the firing squad. Goya's painting of *The Third of May, 1808,* under a midnight sky, is a scene of pure horror. On the right stands a faceless row of uniforms and bearskin hats, of leveled muskets with fixed bayonets; on the left, a mass of bleeding, dead, and soon-to-die humanity. By the light of a lantern Goya spotlights the white shirt and outstretched arms, the blazing eyes, of his central figure. Some of the men crowding around him cover their faces. Others roll their eyes in terror. This painting, by its terribly static quality—in such contrast to the frenzied activity in the painting of May Second—conveys the utter panic of the trapped and helpless victims.

So horrifying were the events of May, 1808, that for Goya neither the memory of them nor the intensity of his emotions had dimmed six years later. In 1814 he wrote that he wanted to paint these canvases, two of his most famous, in order "to commemorate with my brush the exploits, the most remarkable and heroic episodes, of our glorious insurrection against the tyrant of Europe." They stand out in the annals of art as perhaps the most powerful historical paintings ever made.

REASONS FOR THE WAR OF 1812

BRADFORD PERKINS

Although America won its independence in 1783, the United States remained a minor player on the world stage compared to the immense powers of Great Britain and France. As Napoléon's armies marched across Europe, the French and the British navies clashed constantly throughout the Atlantic region. Americans were caught in the middle as merchant ships—filled with trade goods bound for Europe—were seized by both sides. In addition, the British navy filled out its ranks by impressment—the kidnapping and forced labor of thousands of American seamen. As Bradford Perkins, a professor of history at the University of Michigan, writes, these outrages eventually led to the War of 1812.

N either [the British defeat at] Yorktown nor the [final] Peace of Paris made American independence secure. During the 1780's the young nation suffered humiliation at British hands while royalist France, midwife at America's birth, treated her as an upstart ingrate and sought to maneuver her as a satellite. Even after the Constitution, many Americans considered the nation an experiment of doubtful permanence. The French Revolutionary wars added to the buffeting America received. France demanded the support of [Americans]; Britain paid little attention to neutral complaints as she wielded her naval power against her enemy. The Washington administration secured American prosperity . . . but only at the cost of ignoring or compromising many claims against England and provoking an undeclared war with France which lasted from 1798 to 1800.

Excerpted from *Prologue to War: England and the United States, 1805–1812*, by Bradford Perkins. Copyright © 1961 The Regents of the University of California. Reprinted by permission of the University of California Press.

By 1805 America could look back upon twenty years of increasing prosperity interrupted only by the mild depression of 1797; . . . the Louisiana Purchase had improved her position; politically and economically she daily gathered strength. These successes had often been obtained at the price of postponing the assertion of many American rights to a later day. . . .

In May, 1803, Franco-British war recommenced. . . . America soon felt the effects of this struggle. . . . For a decade the United States suffered severely at the hands of European belligerents . . . treated as a pawn or a shuttlecock by Britain and France. In the autumn of 1807 a ragged group of frontiersmen, gathered in a wretched little town . . ., put their names to a declaration of American rights in which they asked, "Is national independence a dream?" Far-reaching belligerent invasions of American sovereignty, rights, and honor made a negative answer by no means obvious.

REBUKED BY NAPOLEON

Napoleon seldom showed respect for America. . . . Instead of encouraging America's European trade, which would have benefited him directly and perhaps more quickly involved the United States in war with Britain, from 1807 onward he did everything possible to restrict it. John Armstrong and Joel Barlow, the American ministers at Paris, suffered humiliation at the Emperor's hands, either through active rebuke, condescending cynicism, or (if the American was fortunate) silent neglect. On the question of Spanish Florida, which [Thomas] Jefferson and many of his followers wished to acquire for America, Napoleon clearly showed his cynicism. He shifted his attitude—his actions scarcely had the continuity to be called policy—according to interests of the moment and particularly his estimate as to whether the carrot or the stick would prove most effective with the Americans. The Emperor's subordinates frequently urged him to adopt a more friendly policy toward the United States. Napoleon never considered this necessary.

Not only contempt for America but even more an understandable conviction that the British war was an overriding concern caused Napoleon to subordinate his American policy to efforts to cripple England's economy. Deprived of hope at sea by [skilled British admiral Lord] Nelson, Napoleon believed commercial warfare "the only way to strike a blow at England and force her to peace." Specifically this meant "remorseless war against English merchandise," an effort to destroy her export trade, undermine the [money's] stability, and sometimes to force her to purchase French goods on very unfavorable terms. In November, 1806, an imperial decree issued at Berlin declared the British Isles in blockade (although Napoleon obviously lacked the naval power to enforce his edict) and prohibited all trade with Englishmen or in British merchandise. Vessels coming from British ports were ordered seized. A little more than a year later a second major decree, this time promulgated at Milan, reinforced and expanded the Berlin Decree. Besides reasserting earlier principles, this declaration announced that ships that submitted to British regulations or allowed themselves to be searched at sea by the Royal Navy would be considered to have lost their neutral character and would therefore be subject to confiscation. Since the great Frenchman dominated most of Europe, this attempt to destroy British trade was quite properly called the Continental System. . . .

The Berlin Decree, which baffled some American merchants and alarmed others, was not seriously enforced against them (nor against the British either, for that matter) until the summer of 1807. Then seizures began, and soon . . . French courts gave their stamp of approval. From that time forward Napoleon dealt harshly with American trade. The Milan Decree aimed fully as much at neutrals as it did at Britain. . . . In 1808, on the ostensible ground that, since the Embargo confined American ships to port, all ships flying the American flag must really be British ships in disguise, Napoleon ordered the condemnation of any such vessels that appeared in the ports of his dominions. . . .

COMMERCIAL WARFARE AGAINST THE UNITED STATES

Considering his meager naval power, Napoleon captured a remarkable number of American merchantmen. Most of them fell into his hands when they were unwary enough to enter French ports, others were taken by French ships which eluded the British blockade, and some fell prey to Napoleon's satellites. In 1805 and 1806 American losses to Britain far outnumbered those to France. From the end of 1807 onward there was little to distinguish the two foes of American commerce. In an official report in July, 1812, Secretary of State [James] Monroe stated that Britain had seized 389 American vessels since . . . 1807. . . . Under the Berlin and Milan decrees, Monroe reported, France had seized 307 American vessels. France had also taken 45 ships since allegedly repealing her decrees in 1810, and her satellites were charged with 117 further captures. Monroe had no satisfactory figures on seizures by Spain while she was an ally of Napoleon, but even so his totals showed Napoleon was responsible for the seizure of at least 468 merchantmen. Moreover, the Secretary's report demonstrated that a ship had far better chances of acquittal or release in a

British admiralty court than in a French one.

Napoleon's policy toward American commerce was thus vehemently hostile. . . . The Emperor showed as little respect for America's rights and even less for her political importance than did British leaders. He tried to scourge rather than inveigle America into hostility to England, repeatedly stating that she must suffer at his hands until she effectively resisted English outrages. In effect he attempted to direct the general course of American policy, refusing to admit that the United States had a right to choose passive neutrality. . . .

BRITISH ASSAULTS ON AMERICA

British assaults upon America exceeded Napoleon's in material impact if not in cynicism. Some conflict between Britain and America was inevitable, for, as an English diplomat serving in Washington put it, "The two greatest Commercial Nations in the Globe cannot move in the same Spheres without jostling one another a little; where we were aiming blows at the French Marine, we want Elbow room and these good Neutrals wont give it to us, & therefore they get a few side Pushes which makes them grumble." The Americans, however, felt they were subjected to more than "a few side Pushes." Britain seized hundreds of American merchantmen and interrupted the sale of agricultural produce abroad; she forced American seamen into [naval] service under the [British flag known as the] Union Jack; her Canadian agents [agitated] among Indian tribes resident in the United States; she rejected or ignored American protests. From 1805 to 1812 there was scarcely a moment when a storm did not loom over Anglo-American relations. Naval officers, diplomats, legislators, and statesmen plunged into the fray. Newspaper editors and pamphleteers on both sides of the Atlantic added their bit to the cacophony. . . . In some ways it is surprising that war did not come until 1812.

At no time after the renewal of European war in 1803 did American merchantmen enjoy immunity from British seizure. Secretary Monroe later reported that from 1805 to 1808 the Royal Navy made prize of one American ship every two days. (An American living in England asserted at the time that the real rate was ten per week.) . . . As far as the British were concerned, they insisted as forcefully as before upon their right to decide what American trade should be permitted. They insisted that prosecution of the war against Napoleon must take priority over all other concerns. . . .

British action within sight of the coast particularly irritated Americans. Cruisers mounted an almost continuous blockade until withdrawn a bit in 1812 in a belated effort to lessen American resentment. Off New York, for example, they frequently halted almost every ship leaving the harbor. Sometimes one or two dozen merchantmen awaited British inspection, and even those not sent to admiralty courts for trial often lost a favourable tide, a useful wind, or perhaps even an advantageous market as the result of delay. Even the British consul at New York, who could not be accused of affection for the Americans, urged the navy to exercise restraint. In 1807 the British minister at Washington wrote:

> I am persuaded that more Ill will has been excited . . .
> by a few trifling illegal Captures immediately off this
> Coast and some Instances of insulting Behaviour by
> some of His Majesty's Naval Commanders in the very
> Harbours and Waters of the United States than by the
> most rigid Enforcement of the Maritime Rights of Great
> Britain against the Trade of the United States in other
> Parts of the World. It may easily be conceived to be
> highly grating to the Feelings of an independent Nation to perceive that their whole Coast is watched as
> closely as if it was blockaded, and every Ship coming
> in or going out of their Harbours examined rigorously
> in Sight of the Shore by British Squadrons stationed
> within their Waters.

Kidnapping American Seamen

. . . Like seizures, the impressment of American seamen [into the British navy] increased in 1805 and troubled Anglo-American relations until war came. In coldly economic terms the loss of seamen counted far less than the loss of ships and cargoes, and the recruiting of British seamen by American ships more than balanced the loss of men through impressment. In terms of human rights and national self-respect, impressment posed an extremely serious challenge. "This authorized system of kidnapping upon the ocean," as John Quincy Adams called it, condemned Americans to many years service in the Royal Navy, sometimes even to death in a foreign monarch's battles. The American tar [seaman] could ask aid of "no judge, no jury, no writ of *habeas corpus*." He was forcibly enlisted in the Royal Navy as a result of a decision a boarding officer made as to his citizenship. He knew that even if American representatives learned of his detention his release would probably be long delayed. Occasionally a seaman threatened with impressment mutilated himself, cut off his hand perhaps, to destroy his usefulness to the British; often he endured weeks of intermittent flogging before he consented to take up his assigned tasks on an English man-of-war. In the end the Royal Navy usually had its way.

This practice, so evil in its effect upon individual seamen, had even more serious implications for the nation. No state that permitted crews under its flag to be mustered by a foreign officer, that tolerated detention of its citizens by another nation, could seriously maintain a claim to complete sovereignty. . . . By impressment even more than by seizures Britain challenged America's stature. Replying to . . . complaints that France treated American commerce as badly as Britain did, a Boston newspaper reminded its readers that "there is another atrocity incident solely to Great Britain, of the blackest and most savage complexion, which would alone convict her of being beyond all comparison to the *greatest aggressor.* We refer to the barbarous THEFTS OF AMERICAN CITIZENS!"

Almost all Britons believed impressment vitally necessary. The number of men in the navy rose from 36,000 in 1792 to about 120,000 in 1805. England's merchant marine lost as many men as it could spare, and large numbers of foreigners had to be enlisted in British service. The *Edinburgh Review* estimated that one-eighth of the navy's seamen were foreigners, and the American consul at London claimed that 15,000 Americans were serving in the Royal Navy, although not all Americans were impressed and many claimed as Americans were British subjects according to English law. To maintain the existing level of manpower and above all to discourage desertion to American merchantmen it seemed imperative to make use of impressment. . . .

[Even] America's bitterest enemies . . . recognized that impressment humiliated the United States, particularly since naval officers often acted capriciously or cruelly toward crews mustered for their inspection. . . .

In many ways, then, the young American felt the sovereignty of his nation challenged and her character insulted by Britain. Some challenges suggested an inferiority of status most important in the realm of the spirit. It would be ridiculous to suggest that the impressment of American seamen or the interruption of American trade did not pose a material challenge, to argue that the loss of thousands of men and hundreds of ships had only a symbolic importance. These very tangible pressures played a fundamental part in the coming of war. Still, since the nation could, after all, prosper despite foreign interference, it is most important to recognize the moral implications of the challenges America faced. Britain treated the new republic as if Yorktown had been an incomplete victory. To many . . . independence seemed almost a dream.

1813–1827

CHAPTER 4

General Napoléon Conquers Europe

Albert Sidney Britt III

French Emperor Napoléon I, or Napoléon Bonaparte, was one of the most brilliant generals in history. Seizing control of the French army during the chaos of the French Revolution, Napoléon's troops marched across Italy, Austria, Egypt, Holland, and Switzerland. After naming himself emperor in 1804, Napoléon instituted a series of wars that left France in brief control of most of the European continent. In the following excerpt, military historian Albert Sidney Britt III follows the rise and fall of General Napoléon's military missions.

O f all the conquerors from Charlemagne to Hitler who tried to unite Europe under their rule, Napoleon Bonaparte most nearly succeeded. At its zenith, the Empire he created stretched from the Atlantic coast to the Russian steppe, from the North Sea to the Mediterranean. Nearly a million men died in less than a quarter of a century trying to prove that Napoleon's brand of equality could be won at cannon point. Meanwhile, proud dynasties learned slowly that traditional military practices could not contain the revolutionary ideas and armies that rapidly transformed the old Europe. . . . It hardly needs saying that these spectacular wars will remain a source of instruction and inspiration as long as men strive for change and hunger for power.

The rise and fall of the French Empire was a complex mosaic of events. Bonaparte's sweep to power dominates the story; inevitably, his worshipers have elevated his deeds to legend.

Excerpted from *The Wars of Napoleon,* by Albert Sidney Britt III, West Point Military History Series, Thomas E. Griess, series editor (Wayne, NJ: Avery, 1985). Reprinted by permission of Penguin Putnam and Thomas E. Griess.

However, one must also account for the poor performance of his opponents before discovering how Europe learned from its tormentor and briefly unified itself to overthrow him. This reversal cannot be explained simply by tracing the path of Napoleon's battles. To fully understand the dramatic growth of the military art, one must consider war in context, recognizing the importance of the contemporary shifting human currents. Changes in warfare in Napoleon's time accompanied an abrupt transformation of European society. Napoleon earned his fame because he observed, understood, and exploited those changing forces. He ultimately fell from power, however, because he disregarded the potential of revolutionary change in other countries and in their armies.

THE MAGNETIC POWER OF PERSONALITY

France's major antagonists—England, Austria, Russia, and Prussia—provided a supporting cast of millions on the European stage, and Napoleon was the artist who played only to a crowd. He took his cue from Revolutionary Paris, where the favor of beautiful women helped determine a man's status and bravery became acknowledged as a symbol of equality. Napoleon adapted his own flair for the romantic to this atmosphere to attract enormous popular support. The Revolution had already freed warfare from past constraints by liberating individual talents and making combat more personal. Generalship—the art of command—now rose to overriding importance in European warfare.

Napoleon's generalship is sometimes difficult to analyze. The Emperor himself caused much of the difficulty by his unseemly practice of altering certain facts in his written reports. Half a century later, French archivists followed suit by hunting down and eliminating some of the documents that might have tarnished their hero's reputation. . . . The best way of studying Napoleon is to accept nothing completely without supporting evidence. This should enhance rather than diminish his stature as a commander. One need only be aware of the practical problems in military planning and operations to wonder at the sureness with which Napoleon flung the *Grande Armée* into every corner of Europe. The brilliant intellect tirelessly at work, estimating time and place for the decisive stroke, dazzles . . . today just as it bewildered his enemies—and some of his subordinates—over a century and a half ago. Anyone who knows just a little about morale will never cease to marvel at the magnetic power of the personality that lifted armies out of misfortune and despair, from the early days in Italy to the last desperate hours at Waterloo.

If generalship is the central theme running all through the

Napoleonic epoch, strategy is surely the primary means by which the master worked his art. . . . Napoleon was a natural strategist. He made strategy flexible, adjusting it to the needs of policy, avoiding enemy strength, and capitalizing on the errors of opposing generals. There was a fluid transition between Napoleonic strategy and tactics; the one blended into and directed the other. Battles were anticipated, not feared, and the French Army fought them where it found them. When a major engagement began, usually it was undertaken with the intention that it would prove decisive. Thus, Napoleonic strategy accepted higher risks for the promise of greater gains. Napoleon was like a shrewd speculator who continually reassesses his vulnerabilities in the light of necessities. Later in his career, however, ambition and overconfidence obscured his view of reality; the recurring urge to strike overcame his better instincts and made him into a reckless gambler.

In that age of upheaval, when kings became fugitives, the structure of the military profession shifted uneasily on its aristocratic foundation. For the first time in centuries, the entire tradition of warfare came into question. Before the French Revolution, the Crown had first claim on the loyalty of soldier and officer. After the [Revolution] in France, nobility counted for little, talent for a great deal. To Napoleon, talent consisted mostly of bravery

and initiative. Both were imperative in the conduct of officers and soldiers. . . .

In spite of France's military victories, professionalism failed to mature in the French Army. Napoleon made all the key decisions; he also developed his own estimates and usually dictated to his subordinates. His staff grew in numbers, but he never used it for anything but collecting the information he demanded and communicating his instructions. There was no effective school system designed to train promising young officers for high level command and staff positions. Expertise was sacrificed to improvisation. As long as the Army continued to win, why reform it? (On the other hand, the Emperor continued to pour money into rebuilding the French Navy, which rarely won a battle, and lay rotting in port during most of his wars.) Those armies that were not as fortunate in battle saw cogent reasons for improving on existing systems. In fact, Prussia decided on the bold course of reforming its entire command, staff, and school system—as well as the Government. In the last years of the war, Prussia instituted a new device for control and coordination at brigade, division, corps, and army levels: the General Staff. No other nation attained such efficiency in the employment of military power, although England and Austria could claim that two decades of fighting against French armies substantially improved the professional abilities of their fighting forces.

The evidence is inconclusive on the subject of logistics. Bonaparte fed his ragged Army of Italy off the plains of Lombardy, and his *Grande Armée* in the Danube Valley. But he encountered barren and hostile steppes in eastern Europe, and he never devised a way to forage for ammunition. Although Napoleon appreciated the importance of logistics and worked hard to support his armies, he failed to build an effective logistical system. . . . As the makeup of his army changed later in his career, Napoleon relied more on firepower, and consequently more on logistics. The classic interaction of technology, tactics, logistics, and strategy thus worked to his disadvantage. At the time when he needed strategic freedom most, logistics came home to haunt him. The *Grande Armée* did not freeze in Russia; it starved.

NAPOLEON'S DOWNFALL

No commander has unlimited freedom in the exercise of his art. If logistics, doctrine, or technology do not limit his courses of action, the chances are that policy will. In contrast to Caesar, who shrewdly gauged the nature of his wars, Napoleon ultimately found the political component of war most difficult to manage. In his early campaigns in northern Italy and southern Germany, he accurately appreciated the relationships between European powers and cleverly foresaw the capabilities and possible reactions of each. But as the Empire expanded, and people—as well as governments—became inflamed against him, all of Europe simmered. Napoleon was fortunate to preserve his imperial rule beyond 1809. In that critical year, insurgency smoldered in the Austrian Tyrol and burned in Spain; Prussia stirred and England threatened. While Frenchmen garrisoned opposite ends of an uneasy Europe, Austria chose to move. Only Napoleon's quick reactions . . . saved the Empire from a setback at perhaps its weakest moment. But it was only saved to meet a worse fate in 1812 and 1813, and it was the political overreach of the Emperor, as much as his military mistakes, that hastened its end. The Emperor Napoleon finally gave General Bonaparte a mission beyond the capability of his army. . . .

More than most professional soldiers would care to admit, the "Ghost of Napoleon," . . . has lingered about many a general's campfire and intruded on nearly every twentieth century battlefield. More than a few of the Western World's most celebrated Great Captains have been captivated by Napoleon's brilliance and have emulated his unceasing quest for the great battle designed to bring the enemy to terms. Battle is only one component of war, however, and armies only the more visible performers. In the age of the Democratic Revolution, the people have gradually taken on a more decisive role in national wars. The growing strength of public opinion had already forecast its power in the French Revolution; ultimately, it became the overriding cause of Napoleon's downfall.

THE BLOODY BATTLE OF NEW ORLEANS

RALPH D. PAINE

During the War of 1812 the United States lost nearly every land battle it fought against the British military. The war ended because the U.S. Navy destroyed the British fleet on the Great Lakes. News of the war's end traveled slowly, however, and even after a peace treaty had already been signed, unknowing American troops commanded by Andrew Jackson met with the British forces of Sir Edward Pakenham near New Orleans, Louisiana. In a bloody battle that made a national hero of Jackson, the Americans achieved total victory, killing more than two thousand British "redcoats" while losing fewer than one hundred men. This accidental battle—fought one week after peace was declared—somehow convinced many Americans that Jackson had helped win the war, even though little was changed between the nations at the war's conclusion. By the 1820s, Jackson the war hero was destined to become president. Ralph D. Paine is an author, historian, and well respected authority on the War of 1812.

A British fleet of about fifty sail, carrying perhaps a thousand guns, had gathered for the task in hand. The decks were crowded with trained and toughened troops, the divisions which had scattered the Americans at Bladensburg [Maryland] with a volley and a shout, kilted Highlanders, . . . and brawny Negro detachments recruited in the West Indies. It was such an army as would have been considered fit to withstand the finest troops in Europe. In command was one of England's most brilliant soldiers, General Sir Edward Pakenham. . . . He was the

Reprinted from *The Fight for a Free Sea*, by Ralph D. Paine (New Haven, CT: Yale University Press, 1920).

idol of his officers, who agreed that they had never served under a man whose good opinion they were so desirous of having, "and to fall in his estimation would have been worse than death." In brief, he was a high-minded and knightly leader who had seen twenty years of active service in the most important campaigns of Europe.

It was Pakenham's misfortune to be unacquainted with the highly irregular and unconventional methods of warfare as practiced in America, where troops preferred to take shelter instead of being shot down while parading across open ground in solid columns. Improvised breastworks [barriers to protect gunners] were to him a novelty, and the lesson of [the Revolutionary War battle at] Bunker Hill had been forgotten. These splendidly organized and seasoned battalions of his were confident of walking through the Americans at New Orleans as they had done at Washington. . . .

ROUGH-AND-TUMBLE WARRIORS

Stranger than fiction was the contrast between the leaders and between the armies that fought this extraordinary battle of New Orleans when, after the declaration of peace, the United States won its one famous but belated victory on land. [If he would have been deployed earlier] on the northern frontier such a man as Andrew Jackson might have changed the whole aspect of the war. He was a great general with the rare attribute of reading correctly the mind of an opponent and divining his course of action, endowed with an unyielding temper and an iron hand, a relentless purpose, and the faculty of inspiring troops to follow, obey, and trust him in the last extremity. He was one of them, typifying their passions and prejudices, their faults and their virtues, sharing their hardships as if he were a common private, never grudging them the credit in success.

In the light of previous events it is probable that any other American general would have felt justified in abandoning New Orleans without a contest. In the city itself were only eight hundred regulars newly recruited and a thousand volunteers. But Jackson counted on the arrival of the hard-bitted, Indian-fighting regiments of Tennessee who were toiling through the swamps with their brigadiers, Coffee and Carroll. The foremost of them reached New Orleans on the very day that the British were landing on the river bank. Gaunt, unshorn, untamed were these rough-and-tumble warriors who feared neither God nor man but were glad to fight and die with Andrew Jackson. In coonskin caps, buckskin shirts, fringed leggings, they swaggered into New Orleans, defiant of discipline and impatient of restraint, hunting knives in their belts, long rifles upon their shoulders. There they drank with seamen as wild as themselves who served in the ships of Jackson's small naval force or had offered to lend a hand behind the stockades, and with lean, long-legged Yankees from down East, swarthy outlaws who sailed for [French pirate] Pierre Lafitte, Portuguese and Norwegian wanderers who had deserted their merchant vessels, and even Spanish adventurers from the West Indies.

The British fleet disembarked its army late in December after the most laborious difficulties because of the many miles of shallow bayou and toilsome marsh which delayed the advance. A week was required to carry seven thousand men in small boats from the ships to the Isle aux Poix on Lake Borgne chosen as a landing base. Thence a brigade passed in boats up the bayou and on the 23d of December disembarked at a point some three miles from the Mississippi and then by land and canal pushed on to the river's edge. Here they were attacked at night by Jackson with about two thousand troops, while a war schooner shelled the British left from the river. It was a weird fight. Squads of Grenadiers, Highlanders, Creoles, and Tennessee backwoodsmen blindly fought each other in the fog with knives, fists, bayonets, and musket butts. Jackson then fell back while the British brigade waited for more troops and artillery.

On Christmas Day Pakenham took command of the forces at the front now augmented to about six thousand, but hesitated

American troops, under the command of Andrew Jackson, achieved total victory in the Battle of New Orleans.

to attack. And well he might hesitate, in spite of his superior numbers, for Jackson had employed his time well and now lay entrenched behind a parapet, protected by a canal or ditch ten feet wide. With infinite exertion more guns were dragged and floated to the front until eight heavy batteries were in position. On the morning of the 1st of January the British gunners opened fire and felt serenely certain of destroying the rude defenses of cotton bales and cypress logs. To their amazement the American artillery was served with far greater precision and effect by the sailors and regulars who had been trained under Jackson's direction. By noon most of the British guns had been silenced or dismounted and the men killed or driven away. "Never was any failure more remarkable or unlooked for than this," said one of the British artillery officers. General Pakenham, in dismay, held a council of war. It is stated that his own judgment was swayed by the autocratic Vice-Admiral [Alexander] Cochrane who tauntingly remarked that "if the army could not take those mud-banks, defended by ragged militia, he would undertake to do it with two thousand sailors armed only with cutlases and pistols."

PREPARING FOR BATTLE

Made cautious by this overwhelming artillery reverse, the British army remained a week in camp, a respite of which every hour was priceless to Andrew Jackson, for his mud-stained, haggard men were toiling with pick and shovel to complete the ditches and log barricades. They could hear the British drums and bugles echo in the gloomy cypress woods while the cannon grumbled incessantly. The red-coated [British] sentries were stalked and . . . ambushed by the Indian fighters who spread alarm and uneasiness. Meanwhile Pakenham was making ready with every resource known to picked troops. . . .

It was Pakenham's plan to hurl a flank [sidelong] attack against the right bank of the Mississippi while he directed the grand assault on the east side of the river where Jackson's strength was massed. To protect the flank, Commodore Patterson of the American naval force had built a water battery of nine guns and was supported by eight hundred militia. Early in the morning of the 8th of January twelve hundred men in boats, under the British Colonel Thornton, set out to take this west bank as the opening maneuver of the battle. Their errand was delayed, although later in the day they succeeded in defeating the militia and capturing the naval guns. This minor victory, however, was too late to save Pakenham's army which had been cut to pieces in the frontal assault.

Jackson had arranged his main body of troops along the inner edge of the small canal extending from a levee to a tangled swamp. The legendary cotton bales had been blown up or set on fire during the artillery bombardment and protection was furnished only by a raw, unfinished parapet of earth and a double row of log breastworks with red clay tamped between them. It was a motley army that Jackson led. Next to the levee were posted a small regiment of regular infantry, a company of New Orleans Rifles, a squad of dragoons [mounted infantrymen] who were handling a howitzer, and a battalion of Creoles in bright uniforms. The line was extended by the freebooters [pirates] of Pierre Lafitte, their heads bound with crimson kerchiefs, a group of American bluejackets, a battalion of Blacks from San Domingo, a few grizzled old French soldiers serving a brass gun, long rows of tanned . . . Tennesseans, more regulars . . . , and rank upon rank of homespun hunting shirts and long rifles, John Adair and his savage Kentuckians, and, knee-deep in the swamp, the frontiersmen who followed General Coffee to death or glory.

A spirit of reckless elation pervaded this bizarre and terrible little army, although it was well aware that during two and a half years almost every other American force had been defeated by an enemy far less formidable. The anxious faces were those of the men of Louisiana who fought for hearth and home, with their backs to the wall. Many a brutal tale had they heard of these war-hardened British veterans whose excesses . . . were notorious and who had laid waste the harmless hamlets of Maryland. All night Andrew Jackson's defenders [waited] until the morning mist of the 8th of January was dispelled and the sunlight flashed on the solid ranks of British bayonets no more than four hundred yards away.

PAYING OFF OLD SCORES

At the signal rocket the enemy swept forward toward the canal, with companies of British [soldiers] bearing scaling ladders and [bundles] of sugar cane. They moved with stolid unconcern, but the American cannon burst forth and slew them until the ditch ran red with blood. With cheers the invincible British infantry tossed aside its heavy knapsacks, scrambled over the ditch, and broke into a run to reach the earthworks along which flamed the sparse line of American rifles. Against such marksmen as these there was to be no work with the bayonet, for the assaulting column literally fell as falls the grass under the keen scythe. The survivors retired, however, only to join a fresh attack which was rallied and led by Pakenham himself.

He died with his men, but once more British pluck attempted

the impossible, and the Highland brigade was chosen to lead this forlorn hope. That night the pipers wailed . . . for the mangled dead . . . who lay . . . with their faces to the foe. This was no Bladensburg holiday, and the despised Americans were paying off many an old score. Two thousand of the flower of Britain's armies were killed or wounded in the few minutes during which the two assaults were so rashly attempted in parade formation. Coolly, as though at a prize turkey shoot on a tavern green, the American riflemen fired into these masses of doomed men, and every bullet found its [target]. . . .

An armistice was granted next day and in shallow trenches the dead were buried, row on row, while the muffled drums rolled in honor of three generals, seven colonels, and seventy-five other officers who had died with their men. Behind the log walls and earthworks loafed the unkempt, hilarious heroes of whom only seventy-one had been killed or hurt, and no more than thirteen of these in the grand assault which Pakenham had led. "Old Hickory" [Jackson] had told them that they could lick their weight in wildcats, and they were ready to agree with him.

Magnificent but useless, after all, excepting as a proud heritage for later generations and a vindication of American valor against odds, was this battle of New Orleans which was fought while the . . . ship, *Astrea*, . . . was driving home to the [United States] with the news that a treaty of peace had been signed at Ghent. With a sense of mutual relief the United States and England had concluded a war in which neither nation had definitely achieved its aims. The treaty failed to mention such vital issues as the impressment of seamen and the injury to commerce by means of paper blockades, while on the other hand England relinquished its conquest of the Maine coast and its claim to military domination of the Great Lakes. English statesmen were heartily tired of a war in which they could see neither profit nor glory. . . . The reverses of first-class British armies at Plattsburg [New York], Baltimore, and New Orleans had been a bitter blow to English pride. Moreover, British commerce on the seas had been largely destroyed by a host of Yankee privateers, and the common people in England were suffering from scarcity of food and raw materials and from high prices. . . . And although the terms of peace were unsatisfactory to many Americans, it was implied and understood that the flag and the nation had won a respect and recognition which should prevent a recurrence of such wrongs as had caused the War of 1812.

THE MIRACLE OF THE ERIE CANAL

LIONEL D. WYLD

The Erie Canal was an engineering and construction miracle of its day, winding through New York State and connecting the Great Lakes to the Atlantic Ocean. Although it was only four feet deep and forty feet wide, the canal required the blood, sweat, and toil of thousands of mostly Irish immigrant workers who carved the ditch through hundreds of miles of virgin hardwood forests and malarial swamps. Historian and author Lionel D. Wyld explains the importance of the canal to the growing prosperity of the United States in the early 1820s.

C onstruction of the Erie Canal began on the Fourth of July, 1817. The site chosen—Rome, New York—was a wise one, for there the digging was easy and the greatest progress could be made in the shortest time. . . . When completed, the canal ran 363 miles from Albany to Buffalo; in this distance eighty-three locks compensated for the various levels, twenty-seven of them in the first fifteen miles or so between Albany and Schenectady around the Cohoes Falls. At Lockport the famous *combines*—five pairs of double-locks—were the marvel of the engineering world; but the dimensions of the canal channel itself, compared with its length and the immensity of the over-all task, seem, in retrospect, almost negligible—40 feet [wide] on the surface, 28 at bottom, with a depth of water to but four feet. It seemed to be little more than a wet ditch, yet it was indeed, as one enthusiastic historian of the canal . . . put it, "from the beginning a golden cord, a bind, in our national existence."

The achievement of this Erie Canal becomes even more remarkable when one considers the state of engineering in this country in 1815. Civil engineering as a profession was unknown. To a large extent, also, the Erie project created the over-all profession of engineering in the United States. With ingenuity matched only by pioneering courage, the Erie engineers coped successfully with countless problems and overcame numerous difficulties. A legislative report in 1958 put their story in romantic and enthusiastic tones:

> The whole question of hydraulics and locks, a waterproof cement, a stump puller and men who could stand the damp and disease of the Montezuma swamps had to be solved. . . . The rock-cutting through the mountain ridge near Lockport was accomplished by DuPont's new blasting powder; the swift waters of the Genesee spanned by a waterbridge of Roman arches; on the 70-foot embankment over the Irondequoit Valley was seen "the sublime spectacle of boats gliding over the hill tops"; hordes of bog-trotting Irishmen left their famine-stricken island to dig in waist-deep mud and water through the mosquito and malaria infested Montezuma marshes; the Mohawk River was crossed by two mighty aqueducts, the Schoharie Creek by a dam crossing; and finally, the level of the Hudson was reached by a flight of 16 locks.

The engineering lay largely in the hands of a few relatively untutored and almost completely inexperienced men. Three names are prominent in this early canal history: James Geddes, Benjamin Wright, and Canvass White. Geddes and Wright had a little surveying in their backgrounds. White went to England where he walked along two thousand miles of towpaths to study English canal construction. "Few men," remarked the president of the American Society of Civil Engineering in 1882, "have ever accomplished so much with so little means."

THE GREATEST CELEBRATION

The Erie Canal opened officially on October 25, 1825, and the ensuing events celebrating the occasion have become an important part of Erie legendry. Not the least were the cannon, placed the length of the canal and down the Hudson River to New York, to carry by successive firings the news of the canal's opening from Buffalo to Manhattan. The festivities ended in New York City on November 4, 1825, when the triumphant procession of canal boats reached New York harbor and were welcomed with one of the greatest spectacle displays in American history.

The Aquatic display transcended all anticipations, twenty-nine steam-boats, gorgeously dressed, with barges, ships, pilot-boats, canal-boats, and the boats of the Whitehall firemen, conveying thousands of ladies and gentlemen, presented a scene which cannot be described. Add to this, the reflections which arise from the extent and beauty of our Bay—the unusual calmness and mildness of the day—the splendid manner in which all the shipping in the harbour were dressed, and the movement of the whole flotilla. Regulated by previously arranged signals, the fleet were thrown at pleasure, into squadron or line, into curves or circles. The whole appeared to move as by magic.

This was written by Cadwallader D. Colden, whom the city fathers had charged with preparing an appropriate *Memoir* for the occasion, a monumental work in its own right, and one which remains important as a repository of contemporary accounts and commentaries of the canal as well as of the celebration which feted its completion.

THE WEDDING OF THE WATERS

The *Seneca Chief*, with [New York City mayor] DeWitt Clinton and a highly diversified cargo aboard, led the cavalcade down the Erie Canal from Buffalo. On board as it left for Albany and New York was a cargo of . . . white fish, from Lake Erie; flour and butter, from Michigan, Ohio, and Buffalo; and some bird's eye maple, and cedar wood, ordered by the Corporation of the City of New York (to make boxes to hold the medals to be struck for the occasion). The [boat] *Young Lion of the West* carried flour, butter, apples, cedar tubs and pails "of very excellent workmanship," some new brooms "of a superior quality," and a deckside menagerie of wolves, foxes, raccoons, and other forest life. The entourage, escorted from Albany by a fleet of steamers, arrived in New York City on November 4, where a gala fete had been arranged in reception. Two kegs of water had been brought from Lake Erie, the contents of one of which was ceremoniously poured into the Atlantic at Sandy Hook. This now-famous "Wedding of the Waters" ceremony, in the words of DeWitt Clinton, was

intended to indicate and commemorate the navigable communication which has been accomplished between [the Great Lakes] and the Atlantic Ocean in about eight years, to the extent of more than [360] miles, by the wisdom, public spirit and energy of the people of the State of New York; and may the God of the Heavens and of the Earth smile most propitiously

on this work and render it subservient to the best interests of the human race.

Then, Dr. Sam Mitchell poured forth into the sea the bottled waters from every part of the globe—the Nile, Ganges, Indus,
Thames, Seine, Rhine, Mississippi, Columbia, Orinoco, and La
Plata—symbolically opening commercial intercourse with all the
nations of the world.

THE START OF THE CANAL ERA

When the canal opened, England had more than a hundred
canals, but no one canal independent of branches extended a
hundred miles. Russia had a 4,500-mile water route, including
lakes, but no one canal reached more than half the length of the
Erie. France's then-famed Languedoc Canal, impressive as it was,
stretched a mere 115 miles. In America, the "Canal Era" began in
earnest. Building canals became an overnight mania. Pennsylvania developed a network of them into the largest system in the
country, but the Erie remained the longest, and the most successful. Every state revived half-completed projects, or turned
previously desultory efforts into enthusiastic ventures in canal
engineering. "All of them," recalled [historian] Edward Everett
Hale in his *Memories of a Hundred Years*, "took on new life with
the triumphant success of the Erie Canal."

The . . . canal's steady and prideful growth from a mere ditch
became an important part of New York State history, with an almost incalculable influence. Freight rates dropped to one-tenth
of what they had been—and even lower. Business boomed all
along the towpath. Within a decade after its opening, the Erie
Canal had paid revenue into the state treasury exceeding the initial outlay for its building . . . and the canal had increased the
value of real estate in New York State by millions of dollars.

Although the canal was not made to accommodate passenger
traffic, early Erie history is filled with travellers' tales; and packet
boats—the "aristocrats of the Old Erie," as Edward Hungerford
called them—cut a fancy pace through central New York. They
offered the tourist or other traveller an inexpensive, leisurely
mode of conveyance. One of the popular guidebooks of the times
gave the following "Description of a Canal Packet Boat" in 1828:

> The length is 60 or 70 feet, a large part of which is de-
> voted to the dining room, where two rows of tables are
> set. At night, mattresses are spread on the seats each
> side, and another row above them on cots suspended
> from the roof. The ladies are accommodated with
> births [*sic*] in the cabin, which is usually carpeted,

hung with curtains, and in other respects more hand-
somely furnished. The kitchen and bar are conve-
niently situated; and the tables are spread with an
abundance, and often a delicacy, which may well surprise those not accustomed to the cheapness of travel-
ling in this part of the country.

A small library, a number of newspapers, &c. will serve
to make the time pass agreeably, even if the traveller be
a stranger, or the weather not inviting. In many places,
the view from the deck is highly interesting. . . .

The heyday of the packet boat was relatively brief, however, for
the stage coaches, though they rocked and pitched, made far better time than did the boaters going their couple of miles an hour.
More particularly, of course, railroad trains seemed to foredoom
the Erie from the very beginning. . . . During its first forty years
the Erie Canal made transportation and commercial history, and
for a short time after the Civil War, in the early 1870's, freight traffic gave the Grand Canal a period of its greatest use. The subsequent decline, despite the abolition of tolls in 1882 and the fervent support of faithful canal backers, came about inevitably.
Railroad mania proved to be as infectious a malaise as had canal
building; the Iron Horse permanently supplanted the canal boat.

SIMÓN BOLÍVAR: LIBERATOR OF SOUTH AMERICA

HAROLD A. BIERCK JR.

As the single most important revolutionary in South America, Simón Bolívar is considered "the Father of Democracy" in Venezuela, Colombia, Ecuador, Peru, and Bolivia. Inspired by the words of seventeenth- and eighteenth-century European philosophers and the deeds of the American revolutionaries, Bolívar struggled against the odds for decades to throw off the repressive chains of Spanish authority in South America. Harold A. Bierck Jr., a respected authority on South American history, gives perspective to the struggles of the man known as "Liberator."

===

S imón José Antonio de la Santisima Trinidad Bolívar was born on July 24, 1783, in Caracas, Venezuela; he died on December 17, 1830, at the Villa San Pedro Alejandrino near Santa Marta, Colombia. Proclaimed "Liberator" by his own people, he was a world-renowned figure in his day. His prophetic vision of hemispheric solidarity lives today, and his political thinking serves dictator and democrat alike in contemporary Latin America. Bolívar has no parallel among the leaders of the United States. The military prowess of Washington, the political views of Jefferson, the humaneness of Lincoln—all can be found in varying measure in the heart, the writings, and the deeds of the Liberator. . . .

The Bolívarian era was fraught with greed and stained with blood. Cries for justice and liberty resounded over a land con-

Reprinted from *Selected Writings of Bolívar*, compiled by Vicente Lecuna, edited by Harold A. Bierck Jr., translated by Lewis Bertrand (Cartagena: Banco de Venezuela, 1951).

fused by social and economic inequalities born of a colonial existence that favored birth over initiative. In 1810 a minority group of propertied white men, obsessed by the magic of independence, began their struggle to break a pattern of life that had been molded by more than three centuries of political restrictions, economic handicaps, and social barriers. These men of property, of whom Bolívar was one, attempted the impossible. The life, liberty, and happiness that they sought to gain through the adoption of a political structure similar to that of the United States had become, by 1830, more a fantasy than a reality. The ideal of freedom was never relinquished, yet realism was the true victor. Lack of experience in democratic government, illiteracy, ill-chosen foreign debts, a temperament that made compromise difficult, the continuance of social inequalities based on birth and property—all combined, as Bolívar prophesied, to prolong the disrupting force of revolution. From this vortex, nevertheless, there emerged a personal dignity, a state of mind, a conviction, a driving force that can only be termed democracy—Latin American democracy. This democracy is epitomized in the writings of Bolívar. Its comprehension by the people of the United States will be the reasoned answer to Latin American political disturbances.

SCHOOLED IN PHILOSOPHY

Within the framework of colonial restriction and revolutionary ferment Bolívar was born, raised, and honored. His life, prior to the beginning of his public career in 1810, was somewhat typical of the wealthy young white of his day. Although he was orphaned at the age of nine (his father died when he was three) his maternal uncle Esteban Palacios cared for his extensive properties and provided him with tutors. Among the latter was Simón Rodríguez. This eccentric disciple of the eighteenth-century Enlightenment schooled the young Bolívar in the precepts of [John Locke, Thomas] Hobbes, and the French *philosophes* [philosophers], particularly [Jean-Jacques] Rousseau. The concepts and principles that were reborn in the Age of Reason were never to be abandoned by Bolívar. Indeed, in his writings the political philosophy of the Enlightenment frequently outweighs his praise of British [parliamentary government] and his criticism of United States federalism.

At the age of sixteen Bolívar went to Spain. In Madrid his wealth procured for him the finest clothes and further education, but his American birth was a handicap to success in the court life of the Spanish capital. . . . After spending several months in Paris the nineteen-year-old Bolívar, deeply in love, returned to Madrid in 1802 and married María Teresa Rodríguez del Toro, daughter of a Caracas-born nobleman. In the summer of that year he brought his bride to Caracas, resigned, apparently, to assume the life of a landed gentleman. But within six months María Teresa died, leaving him childless. Vowing never to remarry, Bolívar returned to Europe, determined to live life to the full.

After a brief visit in Madrid, Bolívar journeyed to Paris, where, with an intensity that characterized his every effort, he gambled, loved, and studied. . . . Bolívar [also] became acquainted with the social life of imperial France. But the glamour of the Napoleonic capital appeared tarnished to the young man of Caracas, and he came to regard the Emperor Napoleon as a dishonored tyrant who had betrayed the principles of French republicanism. His mind, filled with ideas of freedom, liberty, and human rights gained from an avid reading of the works of Montesquieu, Voltaire, Rousseau, Locke, [Etienne de] Condillac, [Georges-Louis de] Buffon, [Jean Le Rond de] D'Alembert, [Claude-Adrien] Helvitius, Hobbes, and [Baruch] Spinoza, found monarchy and its trappings repugnant; hence, he turned to his former tutor, Rodríguez, for advice and intellectual stimulation.

Under the guidance of Rodríguez, or Robinson as he occasionally called himself, Bolívar became a republican in spirit and purpose. "You molded my heart for liberty, justice, greatness, and beauty. . . . You cannot imagine how deeply engraved upon my heart are the lessons you taught me. Never could I delete so much as a comma from the great precepts that you set before me," Bolívar wrote his mentor in later life. In 1805 master and pupil journeyed to southern France and then to Italy. In Rome, on the Monte Sacro, Bolívar vowed that he would liberate his native land. Whether or not this was but an impulse of the moment or the result of mature reasoning cannot be determined from the evidence at hand. It cannot be denied, however, that the remainder of his life was devoted to the fulfillment of that vow. Leaving Rodríguez in Italy, Bolívar returned to Paris, . . . then set sail for the United States. Early in 1807, he visited Boston, New York, Philadelphia, and Charleston. By February of that year he had arrived in Caracas.

WAR FOR INDEPENDENCE

The years 1807–1810 saw the initiation of the Spanish-American Independence movement. Its birthplace was Caracas; one of its children was Bolívar. Aroused by the inequalities of the colonial system, incited by revolutionists like Francisco de Miranda, and angered by the Napoleonic invasion of Spain in 1808, a determined, republican-minded group in Caracas began a series of revolts that ultimately resulted in independence. In 1808, the

people and the colonial authorities of
Caracas rejected Joseph Bonaparte as
King of Spain, and in April, 1810, the
colonial governor was deposed and a
junta [political council] independent
of [Spain] was established.

Bolívar secretly, and in 1809 pub-
licly, participated in these developments. Meetings with other spirited
young men were held at his home in
Caracas in 1808 when agitation for
revolution and independence was rife.
After the arrest of some of the con-
spirators Bolívar withdrew to his
country estate, but in April, 1810, he

Simón Bolívar

and his only brother Juan Vicente openly supported the extrem-
ists who were insisting on the expulsion of the colonial rulers. Two
months later Bolívar was promoted to the rank of colonel in the
militia and appointed head of a diplomatic mission to London. . . .

The War for Independence in northern South America involved a maze of minor actions, attacks and counterattacks,
raids, and lootings, culminating in major battles in which one to
ten thousand men were engaged on each side. Bolívar, as a general, is remembered today chiefly because of his victories in battle, although his writings graphically describe the minutae of the
warfare of his day. From the standpoint of success, Bolívar's military achievements from 1810 to 1818 were temporary only. Lack-
ing organization and equipment, his troops could not maintain
the momentary advantages obtained over a combination of regular Spanish troops, royalist sympathizers, and the fierce *llaneros*,
or Venezuelan plainsmen. . . .

In 1819, convinced of the futility of ousting the enemy from
their Venezuelan strongholds, Bolívar and his aides conceived
the audacious plan of crossing the Andes into New Granada
[present-day Colombia], and, so to speak, attacking the Spanish
from the rear. The wisdom of this plan was proved with the defeat of the royalist army at Boyacá, on August 7, 1819. The victory was the catalyst needed to stir the populace which had been
suffering under the Spanish yoke. After taking Bogotá, Bolívar
returned to free his native land. . . . During a period of truce, he
mapped out several campaigns and personally directed the one
which culminated in victory at Carabobo on June 24, 1821, and
in the reoccupation of Caracas four days later. . . .

With the establishment of the Republic of Grand Colombia in
October, 1821, [Bolívar] the Liberator initiated a series of military

undertakings which, by 1826, resulted in the freeing of Ecuador, Perú, and Bolivia. On April 7, 1822, at Bomboná in western Colombia, Bolívar was again victorious; his ablest lieutenant, General Antonio José de Sucre, enjoyed a like success at Pichincha [Ecuador] on May 24 of the same year. These victories liberated Ecuador, and Bolívar entered Guayaquil on July 11, 1822. Fifteen days later he met General José de San Martín, the liberator of Chile and the Protector of Perú. . . . San Martín expressed complete satisfaction with his army in Perú as he was confident that it would defeat the Spaniards in that area. Bolívar, however, viewed the Peruvian situation in a different light. On September 9, 1822, he dispatched a communication to the governments of Perú and Chile in which he mentioned San Martín's optimism but expressed his own fears for the fate of Perú. He concluded the communication by offering to send 4,000 troops to the aid of Perú. Time justified Bolívar's views respecting the fate of Perú, for the army left by San Martín on his retirement was decisively defeated. Following this defeat Bolívar proceeded to Perú to free that region which San Martín and his aids had failed to accomplish.

Faced with divided loyalties among the Peruvian leaders and compelled to rely largely upon Colombia for troops and supplies, Bolívar undertook the defeat of the Spanish royalists in Perú and Upper Perú, present-day Bolivia. On August 4, 1824, he won his first major victory in that area at Junín. A second and final victory was gained by Sucre at Ayacucho on December 9, 1824. Except for the war between Colombia and Perú in 1829, Bolívar's military career came to an end in 1825. Persistence, untiring zeal, and a depth of purpose coupled with an openly admitted desire for glory enabled him to free five nations. The glory was his, but for this he sacrificed his health, made many enemies, and failed to carry out his plans respecting government. . . .

WIDESPREAD POLITICAL IGNORANCE

Bolívar fervently believed in democracy, yet . . . he, like many other statesmen of Colombia, [recognized] the lack of political experience on the part of the people. Few, too few, were even acquainted with parliamentary procedure; and virtually none possessed an appreciation for compromise, so vital to the operation of the United States and English systems of democracy. A constitution could not, in his opinion, change political concepts and practices molded by three centuries of royal government. His political system was primarily one of paternalism [benevolent, controlling authority]. He envisioned a transitional period during which the people would be educated for complete democracy. History has proved the validity of his views. But many of his contemporaries claimed he sought a crown—a charge unwarranted by the evidence at hand.

Failure rather than success marked Bolívar's efforts in the realm of governmental structures. Bolivia and Perú alone adopted his life-term constitution. This plan of government was rejected in his own country in 1826 and again in 1828 as were many of his political innovations, such as a hereditary senate and a board of censors. . . . Viewed in the historical perspective, his greatest political opponent was the United States Constitution of 1787. Bolívar's own words are proof of this statement. Time and time again he pleaded with congressional delegates and friends not to adopt many of the features of that instrument of government. The colonial political experience of the United States citizen, he repeated, was utterly different from that of the Spanish-American of the day. Time and time alone together with a truly patriotic guidance could prepare the people of Colombia for full participation in their government.

Bolívar was not above dictatorship. In 1827, compelled by circumstances compounded of national debt, civil war, and personal animosities, he assumed dictatorial powers in keeping with the Constitution of 1821. This move, born of a break between the Liberator and Francisco de Paula Santander, Vice President of Colombia, is more to be regretted than debated. Their parting, in 1827, led to a political schism that caused much bloodshed in the years that followed. Perhaps, if the times had not been so turbulent, Bolívar's insistence on a highly centralized government could have been reconciled with Santander's concept of a national state. The failure of these two leaders to agree was responsible for the dictatorship of 1827, an attack on Bolívar's life, exile for Santander, and the creation of two parties in New Granada that were to battle many times subsequent to 1829. Such is the stuff of revolutions.

Failure, however, is not always synonymous with defeat. Time, aided by many a historian, has rendered a different verdict in regard to Bolívar's political achievements, for few will deny that his thoughts and plans of government form the basis of contemporary Spanish-American political thought. The sum total of his theories—their practicality, their eclecticism, yes, even their inconsistencies—stand out today as a tower of wisdom midst the woeful political ignorance of his era. In spite of his faults, he was a political martyr engendered of colonial adolescence in the field of government and enraptured by the paeans to the United States, English, and French democratic-republican systems. At the close of his career he wrote:

I do not expect well-being for the country. This feeling,

or rather this inner conviction, quenches my desire and drags me to the most miserable depths of desperation. I believe all lost forever and the country and my friends submerged in a tempest of calamities. If there were only one more sacrifice that I could make, if it were of my life, my happiness, and my honor, be sure that I would not hesitate. But I am convinced that the sacrifice would be in vain, because one poor man can do nothing against a whole world, and because I am unable to bring about the happiness of my country, I deny myself its command. There is yet more, the tyrants of my country have deprived me of it and I am an exile; so that I do not even have a fatherland for which to make the sacrifice.

Bolívar Ponders Colombian Independence

Simón Bolívar

Simón Bolívar was revered by millions as the great liberator and father of South American democracy. Bolívar, however, did not think the newly independent Colombia—formerly ruled for centuries by a strict Spanish monarchy—could function with a democracy styled after the United States. In the following excerpt, Bolívar explains why he thinks a "president for life"—a dictator— would better serve the Colombian people.

L et us suppose that the Constituent Congress, to be assembled in January, will be wise enough to undertake successful legislative reforms. What might these be? Consider the size of Colombia, her population, the prevailing spirit, the trend of opinions today, the continent in which she is located, the bordering states, and the widespread resentment to the establishment of a stable order. We thus face a chain of fearsome threats that we cannot ignore. The size of our territory requires one of two entirely different types of government, both of them extremely unfavorable to the country's welfare: Monarchy or general confederation are the only forms suitable for the ruling of this far-flung empire. I cannot even conceive of the possibility of establishing a kingdom in a country which is essentially democratic. The lower and most numerous classes claim their prerogatives, to which they have an incontestable right. Equality before the law is indispensable where physical inequality exists, in

Reprinted from *Selected Writings of Bolívar*, compiled by Vicente Lecuna, edited by Harold A. Bierck Jr., translated by Lewis Bertrand (Cartagena: Banco de Venezuela, 1951).

order that the injustices of Nature can, in some measure, be corrected. Moreover, who would be king in Colombia? No one, as I see it. No foreign prince would accept a throne surrounded by dangers and misery, whereas the generals would be compelled to submit to someone else and to renounce forever the supreme authority. The people, frightened by this innovation, would consider themselves sacrificed to the numerous consequences they would foresee in the structure and foundations of a monarchy. The agitators would rouse the people with deceitful arguments, and their persuasiveness would be irresistible, for everything conspires to make this spectre of tyranny appear odious; its very name strikes terror. The poverty of the country does not permit the establishment of an expensive government, favoring every abuse of luxury and dissipation. The new nobility, indispensable in a monarchy, would stem from the people as a whole, and so it would have all the envy of one group and all the arrogance of the other. No one would patiently endure such an aristocracy, steeped in poverty and ignorance and animated by ridiculous pretensions. Let us speak no more, then, of this chimera.

ORGANIZED ANARCHY

Nevertheless, I am less inclined toward the federal form of government. Such a system is no more than organized anarchy, or, at best, a law that implicitly prescribes the obligation of dissolution and the eventual ruin of the state with all its members. I think it would be better for South America to adopt the Koran rather than the United States' form of government, although the latter is the best on earth. Nothing more can be added; simply witness the unhappy [people in the quasi democratic] countries of Buenos Aires, Chile, Mexico, and Guatemala. We, too, may recall our own earliest years. These examples alone tell us more than entire libraries.

There remains no alternative for Colombia but to organize, as best she can, a centralized system duly proportioned to the size of her territory and the nature of her inhabitants. A civilized state based on the European model offers less resistance to government, on the part of the people and of nature, than does a small province in America, by reason of the ruggedness of our terrain and the ignorance of our people. For these very reasons we are compelled to give our institutions greater stamina and energy than would be considered necessary in other countries. Colombia is not only as large as a European state, but she could hold several nations of Europe within her borders. What problems and obstacles shall we not encounter in administering a far-flung empire when the government is equipped with tools barely sufficient to rule a single province, and that badly?

If I am to speak my mind, let me say that I have seen nothing whatsoever in Colombia resembling government, administration, or public order. It is true that we are beginning a new career, and that war and revolution have directed all our attention toward fighting. We have appeared to be transfixed by the contemplation of our dangers and by the anxiety to avert them. We did not know what it meant to govern, and, while we were engaged in defending ourselves, we did not have the time to learn. But now it is time to think deeply and earnestly of repairing all these losses and insuring our national existence.

The present government of Colombia is not adequate for ruling and administering extensive provinces. The center is too far removed from the outlying sections. Force is dissipated by distance, and the central administration lacks the necessary means to deal with the immensity of its far-reaching responsibilities. I repeatedly observe evidence of this fact. There is no prefect, no governor, who does not invest himself with supreme authority, principally as a matter of absolute necessity. It might be said that each department has a government distinct from the national, modified by local conditions or circumstances peculiar to the area, or even personal in nature. All this exists because the whole is not compact. Our social ties are too loose to stabilize, bind, and hold together the remote sections of our country. We suffer from such utter confusion and we are so incapable of remedying this evil that, unless we reorganize, this disease will make dangerous progress.

A LIFE-TERM PRESIDENT

The Constituent Congress must choose . . . the creation of a life-term presidency and a strong central government. . . .

The formation of a life-term government or any other system that should be desired—but always in accordance with the popular will—is the other possibility that the Congress might adopt. The preservation of the Republic of Colombia offers, of course, genuine advantages and prestige abroad. Spain will have greater respect for us; Peru' will honor any treaties she signs; and the nations of America generally will continue to look up to us. The citizens of both countries will be less inclined to engage in border clashes, and the national debt will offer less occasion for dispute. All this is of great importance. If only we could preserve this beautiful union!

Colombia must forget her illusions and make her decision, for I cannot rule any longer.

1828–1837

CHAPTER 5

POLITICAL TRANSITION IN THE UNITED STATES

GEORGE DANGERFIELD

By the 1820s the United States was growing at an incredible rate. The nation had spread west far beyond the original thirteen states to include rural, mostly undeveloped states such as Kentucky, Tennessee, Ohio, and Indiana. As the men in these regions gained political power (women were not allowed to vote) the control of the U.S. government by East Coast aristocrats was overwhelmed by a new style of democracy as practiced by the seventh president, Andrew Jackson.

As historian and author George Dangerfield explains, Jacksonian democrats believed that the government should act to help the powerless restrain the business practices of wealthy bankers and speculators. This stood in direct opposition to standard government laissez-faire policy of the time, which stated that government should not interfere in business affairs.

A ll historical periods are, it is true, transitional, nor is any transition ever complete. If I have ventured to apply the word "transition" to the period covered by the administrations of James Monroe and John Quincy Adams, it is because this period passes through three quite well-defined phases.

(I) The first two years of Monroe's Presidency were remarkable for a nationalist exuberance, which arose from the fact that the United States had emerged from the encroachments of the Napoleonic Wars, and the perils of the War of 1812, not only safely but also with an increased prestige.

(II) The exuberance which greeted and acclaimed Monroe, however, was sustained and intensified by a land boom and a cotton boom; and when these booms collapsed in 1819, the Era of Good Feelings properly came to an end. There followed a period of deep economic depression. During this period, Americans sought, by all sorts of strange and desperate expedients, to obtain some brief respite from the waters of debt.

(III) The depression lasted at least until 1823; and when good times began slowly to return, the debtor classes had leisure to ask themselves whether they had not been abandoned by the general government in the hour of their need, and whether they should not look for a new kind of general government—one that would promote, by strong action and not by negative precept, the great "agrarian" ideal of a society of independent property-owners.

This ideal was not opposed to sound business enterprise or to a *laissez-faire* economy [in which the government did not interfere in business decisions]; but it insisted that this *laissez-faire* economy should be modified in an "agrarian" manner (that is to say, in favor of the weak, by attacking monopoly wherever it showed its head) rather than in a "capitalist" manner (that is to say, in favor of the strong, by the distribution of subsidies and privileges whenever they were called for). . . . If [Jackson is well-remembered] today, it is not because of his . . . ideal of a society of independent property-owners, but because of his valiant faith in the dignity of the individual, the uncommonness of the common man.

It was during the last years of Monroe's Presidency, and throughout the four years of the Presidency of Adams, that American agrarians began to define their rights and to formulate their grievances. They demanded a wider suffrage, rotation in office, a greater access to the business of government and therefore to the history of their times: they complained of imprisonment for debt, of insufficient public education, . . . of fraudulent banks of issue, of too close a connection between the general government and the moneyed interest. It was by listening to and learning from these demands and grievances that Andrew Jackson, who came to the Presidency in 1829 with no program and almost no ideas, became one of the great popular leaders of American history. . . .

ONE-PARTY GOVERNMENT

The phrase "Era of Good Feelings" has customarily been extended to cover the whole eight years of Monroe's Presidency; not simply because of the nationalism which so distinguished its early years and never vanished from its later ones, but also because it was a period of one-party government. Almost every man called himself a Jeffersonian Republican in those days, and political conflicts on a national scale were apt to be conflicts between personalities and not between principles or programs. This gives the whole period a certain fascination, because the leading personalities were very strong and very brilliant and because they were quite sure, in all but the most . . . secret of their transactions, that what they said and did would be quoted and remembered for generations to come. In this innocent respect, the Era of Good Feelings was pre-eminently the era of the personal myth.

But one-party government cannot continue long in a political democracy without resorting to dictatorship or dissolving into anarchy. It is not flexible, not responsive to the people; it tends to produce a crusty political elite; and it is easily ensnared by any special interest strongly enough organized to make its wishes felt. The rule of the Republican Party under Monroe was seriously shaken by the panic of 1819. . . . From then onwards it tended more and more to become the party of federal subsidies and special privileges, of high protective tariffs and of strong but potentially irresponsible central banking. . . . And so it came about that by the end of Adams's Presidency—itself a curious and instructive example of political anarchy—the old Republican Party was almost completely out of touch with the wishes and aspirations of a majority of the American people. The majority of the American people, therefore, swept Andrew Jackson and his Democrats into office in the election of 1828.

Looking backward from the complexities of our times to the simplicities of those early days, we can at least infer from the administrations of Monroe and Adams, both of them good and sincere men, that good and sincere men may sometimes . . . advocate very dangerous policies, and that they will often do so from the best of motives. If political democracy is to survive, in these times as in those, it must survive by fighting the policies and not by persecuting the men.

ANDREW JACKSON, THE PEOPLE'S PRESIDENT

FREDERIC AUSTIN OGG

By the time of Andrew Jackson's inauguration in 1828, the newly elected seventh president was so popular among average citizens that his swearing-in ceremony generated near hysteria in the streets of Washington, D.C. As historian Frederic Austin Ogg writes, the wild party that followed shocked and stunned the capital's former aristocratic rulers.

Jackson's election to the presidency in 1828 was correctly described by Senator [Thomas H.] Benton as "a triumph of democratic principle, and an assertion of the people's right to govern themselves." [Thomas] Jefferson in his day was a candidate of the masses, and his triumph over John Adams in 1800 was received with great public acclaim. Yet the Virginian [Jefferson] was at best an aristocratic sort of democrat; he was never in the fullest sense a man of the people. Neither [Presidents James] Madison nor [James] Monroe inspired enthusiasm, and for John Quincy Adams even [fellow] New Englanders voted . . . from a cold sense of duty. Jackson was, as no President before him, the choice of the masses. [Although he lost in the electoral college,] his popular vote in 1824 revealed not only his personal popularity but the growing power of the democratic elements in the nation. . . .

The untrained, self-willed, passionate frontier soldier came to power in 1828 as the standard bearer of a mighty democratic uprising which was destined before it ran its course to break down oligarchical party organizations [run only by the privileged], to liberalize state and local governments, and to turn the stream of

Excerpted from *The Reign of Andrew Jackson*, by Frederic Austin Ogg (New Haven, CT: Yale University Press, 1919).

national politics into wholly new channels. It was futile for men of the old school to protest and to prophesy misfortune for the country under its new rulers. The people had spoken, and this time the people's will was not to be denied. . . . The President-elect set out for Washington, at the middle of January, 1829. . . . The puffing little steamboat on which [Jackson] traveled down the Cumberland and up the Ohio was saluted and cheered a hundred times a day; at Louisville, Cincinnati, and Pittsburgh there were great outpourings of demonstrative citizens. . . . As the party passed along the National Road toward its destination it was accorded an ovation which left nothing to be desired as an evidence of the public favor.

SPECULATION AND SPECULATORS

Arrived in Washington, on the 11th of February—the day on which the electoral votes were counted in the Senate—Jackson and his friends found temporary lodgings at the Indian Queen Tavern, commonly known as "the Wigwam." During the next three weeks the old inn was the scene of [uncommon] activity. Office seekers besieged it morning, noon, and night; politicians came to ask favors or give advice; exponents of every sort of cause watched for opportunities to obtain promises of presidential support; scores of the curious came with no other purpose than to see what a backwoods President looked like. "The city is full of speculation and speculators," wrote [Massachusetts senator] Daniel Webster to his sister-in-law a few days after Jackson's arrival; "a great multitude, too many to be fed without a miracle, are already in the city, hungry for office. Especially, I learn that the [news] corps is assembled in great force. . . . So many friends ready to advise, and whose advice is so disinterested, make somewhat of a numerous council about the President-elect; and, if report be true, it is a council which only makes that darker which was dark enough before."

To all, Jackson was accessible. But he was not communicative, and up to Inauguration Day people were left to speculate not only upon the truth of the rumor that there was to be a "full sweep" in the offices but upon the new Administration's attitude on public questions in general. Even Isaac Hill, a warm friend and supporter, was obliged to write to an acquaintance four days before the inauguration that Jackson had little to say about the future, "except in a general way." . . .

THE PEOPLE'S PRESIDENT

Meanwhile a motley army of office seekers, personal friends, and sightseers—to the number of ten or fifteen thousand—poured into Washington to see the old régime of Virginia, New York, and Massachusetts go out and the new régime of the people come in. "A monstrous crowd of people," wrote Webster on Inauguration Day, "is in the city. I never saw anything like it before. Persons have come five hundred miles to see General Jackson, and they really seem to think that the country is rescued from some dreadful danger." Another observer, who was also not a Jacksonian, wrote:

Andrew Jackson

> No one who was in Washington at the time of General Jackson's inauguration is likely to forget that period to the day of his death. To us, who had witnessed the quiet and orderly period of the Adams Administration, it seemed as if half the nation had rushed at once into the capital. . . . The West and the South seemed to have precipitated themselves upon the North and overwhelmed it. . . . Strange faces filled every public place, and every face seemed to bear defiance on its brow. It appeared to me that every Jackson editor in the country was on the spot. They swarmed, especially in the lobbies of the House, an expectant . . . band, which, having borne in upon their shields their idolized leader, claimed the reward of the hard-fought contest.

The 4th of March dawned clear and balmy. "By ten o'clock," says an eye-witness, "the Avenue was crowded with carriages of every description, from the splendid baronet and coach, down to wagons and carts, filled with women and children, some in finery and some in rags, for it was the People's president." The great square which now separates the Capitol and the Library of Congress was in Jackson's day shut in by a picket fence. This enclosure was filled with people—"a vast agitated sea"—while in all directions the slopes of Capitol Hill were thickly occupied. At noon watchers on the west portico, looking down Pennsylvania Avenue, saw a group of gentlemen issue from the Indian Queen and thread its way slowly up the hill. All wore their hats except one tall, dignified, white-haired figure in the middle, who was quickly recognized as Jackson. Passing through the building, the party, reinforced by Chief Justice [John] Marshall and certain other dignitaries, emerged upon the east portico, amid the deafening cheers of the spectators. The President-elect bowed gravely, and, stepping forward to a small cloth-covered table, read in a low voice the inaugural address; the aged Chief Justice, "whose life was a protest against the political views of the Jackson party," administered the oath of office; and the ceremony was brought to a close in the customary manner by the new Executive kissing the Bible. Francis Scott Key [composer of "The Star-Spangled Banner"], watching the scene from one of the gates, was moved to exclaim: "It is beautiful, it is sublime."

Thus far the people had been sufficiently impressed by the dignity of the occasion to keep their places and preserve a reasonable silence. But when the executive party started to withdraw, men, women, and children rushed past the police and scrambled up the steps in a wild effort to reach their adored leader and grasp his hand. Disheveled and panting, the President finally reached a gate at which his horse was in waiting; and, mounting with difficulty, he set off for the White House, followed by a promiscuous multitude, "countrymen, farmers, gentlemen, mounted and unmounted, boys, women, and children, black and white."

The [former] President had no part in the day's proceedings. On arriving in Washington, Jackson had refused to make the usual call of the incoming upon the outgoing Executive, mainly because he held Adams responsible for the news paper virulence which had caused [Jackson's wife] such distress and had possibly shortened her life. Deserted by all save his most intimate friends, the New Englander [Adams] faced the last hours of his Administration in bitterness. His diary bears ample evidence of his ill-humor and chagrin. On the 3d of March he took up his residence on Meridian Hill, near the western limits of the city; and thence he did not venture until the festivities of the ensuing day were ended. No amount of effort on the part of mediators ever availed to bring about a reconciliation between him and his successor.

A WILD PARTY AT THE WHITE HOUSE

According to custom, the inaugural program came to an end with a reception at the White House; and arrangements were made to entertain a large number of guests. Police control, however, proved wholly inadequate, and when the throng that followed the President up the Avenue reached the executive grounds it engulfed the mansion and poured in by windows as well as doors, until the reception rooms were packed to suffocation. Other guests, bidden and unbidden —"statesmen and stable-boys, fine ladies and washerwomen, white people and blacks"—continued for hours to besiege the doors. "I never saw such a mixture," records Judge [Joseph] Story; "the reign of King Mob seemed triumphant. I was glad to escape from the scene as soon as possible." The President, too, after being jostled for an hour, very willingly made his way by a side entrance to the street and thence to his hotel.

A profusion of refreshments, including barrels of orange punch, had been provided; and an attempt to serve the guests led to a veritable saturnalia. Waiters emerging from doors with loaded trays were borne to the floor by the crush; china and glassware were smashed; gallons of punch were spilled on the carpets; in their eagerness to be served men in muddy boots leaped upon damask-covered chairs, overturned tables, and brushed bric-à-brac from mantels and walls. . . . Only when some thoughtful person directed that tubs of punch be placed here and there on the lawn was the congestion indoors relieved. When it was all over, the White House resembled a pigsty. "Several thousand dollars' worth of broken china and cut glass and many bleeding noses attested the fierceness of the struggle." It was the people's day, and it was of no avail for fastidious Adamsites to lift their eyebrows in ridicule or scorn.

THE RAILROAD REVOLUTION

OLIVER JENSEN

The perfection of the steam engine in the late eighteenth century allowed the first railroads to operate in England in 1823. This revolution in transportation technology quickly spread to the United States, and by 1827 the first tracks of the Baltimore & Ohio Railroad were laid down after a boisterous ceremony outside Baltimore, Maryland. As Oliver Jensen, board chairman of the Valley Railroad Company of Essex, Connecticut, writes, America's first great railroad had to overcome several problems before its engines could roll.

O f all the pioneer railroads built in the excitement of the late 1820's and early 1830's, by far the most significant was the Baltimore & Ohio, whose very name proclaimed its vast ambitions. America's third largest city at the time, yet two hundred miles nearer to the western waters than New York and one hundred nearer than Philadelphia, Baltimore was fearful of the competition of New York and her new Erie Canal. Although the city was the starting point for the colorful traffic over the famous National Road, crowded with Concord coaches and Conestoga wagons, farseeing men like Philip Thomas and his brother Evan, who had seen England's new coal-carrying railways, decided that only rails, albeit with only horse-drawn power, could preserve their competitive position.

MUCH TO CHEER ABOUT

The Baltimore & Ohio was chartered with Philip Thomas as president in 1827, and its cornerstone laid amid great parades and re-

Excerpted from *The American Heritage History of Railroads in America*, by Oliver Jensen. Copyright © 1975 American Heritage Publishing Company. Reprinted by permission of American Heritage Inc.

joicings on July 4, 1828. The first spadeful of earth was turned over by the venerable Charles Carroll of Carrollton, then over ninety and the last surviving signer of the Declaration of Independence. As the tradesmen marched smartly by, the floats glided through the streets, and the bands blared, old Mr. Carroll quietly remarked to his friends, "I consider this among the most important acts of my life, second only to my signing the Declaration of Independence, if even it be second to that." Just about that time, the most impressive float of all, a miniature brig named the *Union,* manned entirely by Baltimore shipmasters in natty uniforms, paused before Mr. Carroll.

"Ship ahoy!" cried Carroll's aide. "What is the name of that ship and by whom commanded?"

"The *Union;* Captain Gardner," was the reply.

"From whence came you, and where bound?"

"From Baltimore, bound to the Ohio."

"How will you get over the mountains?"

"We've engaged a passage by the railroad."

Much cheering, no doubt, although it would take twenty-four years to get to the Ohio. But there was much to cheer about, for the Baltimore & Ohio would grow, and last, reaching into thirteen states and most of the largest cities in America. . . .

When the cheering stopped, the Baltimore & Ohio started building; it was, after all, the first railroad of any consequence, and everything had to be learned by trial and error. The first part of the roadbed, following the English model, was built for the ages: solid, level, its rail originally mounted on stone blocks, its bridges, like the Carrollton Viaduct [in Relay, Maryland], masterpieces of masonry which still stand. Most of its construction engineers were famous men—Jonathan Knight, the chief, Stephen H. Long, the western explorer, Major George Washington Whistler, the husband of the lady in his son's famous painting of "Whistler's Mother". . . , his West Point friend Captain William G. O'Neill, and Benjamin H. Latrobe, son of the noted architect of the National Capitol. . . .

Tom Thumb Locomotive

Experimentally at least, steam came to the Baltimore & Ohio before it appeared at Charleston when Peter Cooper, another tinker and inventor cut from much the same plain honest cloth as George Stephenson, appeared on the scene just as progress with the railroad was slowing down. Self-educated, a former carriage maker's apprentice, then a grocer and glue manufacturer, Cooper had bought real estate in Baltimore and started making iron there. How better to protect his investment than to help the city grow? Here is how he told the story himself, fifty-two years later, in the *Boston Herald:*

"The Baltimore & Ohio Railroad had run its tracks down to Ellicott's Mills, thirteen miles, and had laid 'snakehead' rails, as they called them, strap rails, you know, and had put on horses. Then they began to talk about the English experiments with locomotives. But there was a short turn of 150 feet radius . . . and the news came from England that Stephenson said that no locomotive could draw a train on any curve shorter than a 900-foot radius. . . . The directors had a fit of the blues. I had naturally a knack of contriving, and I told the directors that I believed I could knock together a locomotive that would get the train around. . . .

"So I came back to New York and got a little bit of an engine, about one-horse power . . . and carried it back to Baltimore. I got some boiler iron and made a boiler about as big as an ordinary washboiler, and then how to connect the boiler with the engine I didn't know. . . . I had an iron foundry, and had some manual skill in working in it. But I couldn't find any iron pipes. The fact is, there were none for sale in this country. So I took two muskets and broke off the wood part, and used the barrels for tubing to the boiler. . . . I went into a coachmaker's shop and made the locomotive, which I called the 'Tom Thumb,' because it was so insignificant. I didn't intend it for actual service, but only to show the directors what could be done. I meant to show two things; first, that short turns could be made; and secondly, that I could get rotary motion without the use of a crank. . . . I got steam up one Saturday night; the president of the road and two or three gentlemen were standing by, and we got on the track and went out two or three miles. All were delighted, for it opened up new possibilities for the road. I put the locomotive up for the night. All were invited to a ride Monday—a ride to Ellicott's Mills.

"Monday morning, what was my grief and chagrin to find that some scamp had been there and chopped off all the copper from the engine and carried it away, doubtless to sell to some junk dealer. The copper pipe that conveyed the steam to the pistons was gone. It took me a week or more to repair it. Then . . . we started—six on the engine, and thirty-six on the car. It was a great occasion, but it didn't seem so important then as it does now. We went up an average grade of eighteen feet to the mile, and made the passage . . . to Ellicott's Mills in an hour and twelve minutes. We came back in fifty-seven minutes. Ross Winans, the president of the road, and the editor of the Baltimore Gazette made an estimate of the passengers carried, and the coal and water used, and reported that we did better than any English road did for four years after that. The result of the experiment was that the bonds were sold at once and the road was a success."

Peter Cooper did not say a word about the famous race with a horse on the way home, when the stage people hitched a fine grey to a carriage on a parallel track and challenged the *Tom Thumb*. The tiny locomotive was soon in the lead when its primitive blower failed, the fire cooled, and the horse swept by to victory—its last. Popular folklore to the contrary, Peter Cooper was not the father of steam locomotion in America, or even a significant contributor to the science. But he was a picturesque popularizer, and after his demonstration, the Baltimore & Ohio did buy some very practical steam engines for its long struggle to the West.

THE "YOUNG ITALY" MOVEMENT

GIUSEPPE MAZZINI

Napoléon was the king of Italy from 1802 until 1814. The period of French rule temporarily unified Italy and introduced the principles of basic human rights made popular by the French Revolution. Italians felt a swell of national pride and great hope that their country could remain unified and someday experience self-government.

When the French were defeated in the Napoléonic Wars, Italy was divided up between Austria, the Papal States ruled by the pope, the kingdom of Sardinia, and other small autocratic states ruled by petty princes.

When this oppressive rule was restored, freedom-lovers formed the *Risorgimento*, or "revival," movement dedicated to the unity and independence of Italy.

In 1831, Giuseppe Mazzini, a passionate young revolutionary organized the *Giovane Italia*, or, "Young Italy" movement to unify his country. In the excerpt below, written in 1832, Mazzini explains the need for such a movement within the context of Italian history and the 1789 French Revolution.

W e stand at the edge of an era. . . . Forty years of striving, baptism in tears and blood, and the European development that has taken place before our eyes, have borne the fruit of wisdom and courage; and ours is a country which gives unusual swiftness to the talents of her sons, and a quicker beat to their hearts.

We have beheld Europe. Everywhere the cry for new things

has arisen, an appeal to new emotions, a summons to new principles, which the century has put in ferment. Everywhere it is one battle. . . . Unity! We desire it, but unity only among good people, and unity founded on truth. The other kind, which some still call for in their timidity or their folly, without saying how it is to be achieved, is a union of corpses with a living thing; it smothers the light of life in the living, but gives no spark to what is dead.

We have beheld Italy—Italy, the purpose, the soul, the consolation of our thoughts, the country chosen of God and oppressed by men, twice queen of the world and twice fallen through the infamy of foreigners and the guilt of her citizens, yet lovely still though she be dust, unmatched by any other nation whatever fortune has decreed; and Genius returns to seek in this dust the word of eternal life, and the spark that creates the future. We have tried to see her with an objectivity as cool as intense longing and the need to grasp her internal nature will allow—and our hearts beat strong within our breasts, for we have young passions, and pride in the name Italian lifts our souls within—but we enjoined our hearts to silence, and saw her as she was—vast, strong, intelligent, fertile with the elements of rebirth, beautiful in memories such as could create a second universe, peopled with spirits great in sacrifice, and great in victory—but laid to waste, divided, mistrustful, ignorant, wavering irresolute between the threats of tyranny and the treacherous flattery of the many who with their adulation of her antique grandeur put her to sleep lest she seek new grandeur. . . .

And we looked at the past, to see whether we could find the remedy there. Now the past has taught us not to despair, the past has taught us how many things and which things are only artifices of tyranny and relics of servitude of the spirit—no more than that. The learning of our forefathers was exercised more in the realm of principles than of application. Perhaps the flame of fatherland and liberty with which they burned showed them how vast the arena was. But circumstances stifled the conception, and their efforts took on neither the energy, nor the magnitude, nor the harmony that such work requires. Harmony of principles and actions was necessary—and the movements that broke out were partial instead, and provincial. But without a universal movement, triumph will always prove impossible; without the universality of prior accord, the movement will not break out simultaneously, nor ever be truly Italian—and for the envies and the animosities that still exist among the provinces to be erased once and for all, all must be fraternalized in the brotherhood of movement, of danger, of victory. . . . Revolutions are prepared with education, they are matured with care, they are carried out with energy, and they are hallowed by their dedication to the common good. But these most recent revolutions broke out unexpected, unprepared, artificially connected; they aimed at the triumph of one class over another, of a new aristocracy over an old—and no thought was given to the people. Then, they proceeded on the basis of artificial principles, putting the interpretation of them in the hands of astute authorities, frightened of everything, despairing of any help from diplomacy, or from foreigners—the first essentially a dishonest art, the other essentially suspect, useful sometimes for the strong, but never for the weak. We saw men revile kings, setting up laws and agreements that openly showed distrust of them and that limited their power—and at the same time these men put unlimited trust in their promises, as though tyrants had a God in whose name they could swear. We saw the aristocracy attacked in constitutions, and nevertheless called to the summit of affairs, as though this caste could ever commit suicide. We read on the banners the name of Italy, while we saw disowned brothers who had risen nearby in the same cause, in the same hour, in a common effort. We heard the cry of territorial independence, while the barbarian guarded the doors; and meanwhile the policy of the new governors was dominated by the hope of avoiding that war which nature has made eternal between master and slave, which breaks his chains—and youth was curbed when it sought to move into a larger arena—they decreed togas instead of arms. These were errors born of the fault of cowardice on the part of the very ones vilely deceived and betrayed, errors sprung more perhaps from the positions and the infamy of the European cabinets than from those of the men at the head of our affairs, but such that for shrewd politicians of wide experience to persist in them now must be the part of incompetence or of treason.

And then—we looked around ourselves, and then—we launched ourselves into the future. The spirit wearied by long delusions took new heart in the awareness of an eternal mission; it rekindled in the sentiment of patriotic fervor, of the passion for liberty, which is life for us. The errors of the fathers had come from the will of their age; but why should we persist in the errors of the fathers? The years mature new destinies; and we, contemplating the movement of the age, glimpse a new generation, fervent in hope—and hope is fruit in the bud—inspired to new things by the *spiritual* breath of the era, stirred by a pervasive need for strong shocks and sensations. And as a means to create this generation, amid the confusion of the systems, amid the anarchy of principle, from the individualism of the Middle Ages, from the mire in which Italian life is held fast, we saw emerging here and there men who lived and died for an idea. . . .

YOUNG ITALY

It is simply a system, let us say it again, that we have tried to identify with the name *Young Italy;* but we chose this term because the one term seems to marshal before the youth of Italy the magnitude of its duties and the solemnity of the mission that circumstances have entrusted to it, so that it will be ready when the hour has struck to arise from its slumber to a new life of action and regeneration. And we chose it because we wanted to show ourselves, writing it, as what we are, to do battle with raised visors, to bear our faith before us, as the knights of medieval times bore their faith on their shields. For while we pity men who do not know the truth, we despise men who, though they know the truth, do not dare to speak it.

Undefiled by connections or by private grudges, hearts burning with generous wrath but open to love, with no other desire than to die for the progress of humanity and for the liberty of the fatherland, we need not be suspected of personal ambition or of envy. Envy is not one of youth's passions. Who among us cares for individuals? . . . We are in the age of principles; only them do we defend or attack, only on this battlefield are we inexorable. There is the pivot of the future; there stand our dearest hopes. The generations pass; names and the battles that surround them are drowned in the popular torrent, in its flood. We draw a veil over the things that have happened—who can make them not exist? But the future is ours; the theories of the past we refute by the age that presses upon us. We raise our banner between the old world and the new. Let him who will, rally to this banner; let him who will not, live on memories, but let him not seek to resurrect from them another banner, fallen, ragged.

If, among the men whose birth in an era earlier than ours makes them think that we or our principles might exclude them from the movement, there be any who have gray hairs on their heads but enthusiasm in their hearts, men who moving with the times are awake to the progressive unfolding of the revolutionary elements, and who in accordance with this development modify the scope of their activities, oh let them come to us! Let them view dispassionately our theories, our actions, our achievements—and come to us! Come, and bare before us the honorable wounds won in the fields of the fatherland's battles. We shall kiss those holy wounds, we shall venerate those white hairs, we shall accept their counsel, and, rallying around them, we shall display them to our enemies with pride, proclaiming: "We have the voice of the past and that of the future for our cause!". . .

Youth, my brothers—take comfort and be great! Faith in God, in the right, and in ourselves! . . . Raise this cry—and forward! Events will show whether we are mistaken when we say the future is ours.

Restless Americans

Alexis de Tocqueville

Although French author Alexis de Tocqueville extolled the great virtues of the democratic system in the United States, he had a difficult time understanding the American people. In de Tocqueville's view, even the most prosperous people were unhappy with their wealth and seemed feverishly driven to obtain more. In the following excerpt, de Tocqueville ponders this uniquely American conundrum.

n certain remote corners of the Old World you may still sometimes stumble upon a small district which seems to have been forgotten amidst the general tumult, and to have remained stationary whilst everything around it was in motion. The inhabitants are for the most part extremely ignorant and poor; they take no part in the business of the country, and they are frequently oppressed by the government; yet their countenances are generally placid, and their spirits light. In America I saw the freest and most enlightened men, placed in the happiest circumstances which the world affords: it seemed to me as if a cloud habitually hung upon their brow, and I thought them serious and almost sad even in their pleasures. The chief reason of this contrast is that the former do not think of the ills they endure—the latter are forever brooding over advantages they do not possess. It is strange to see with what feverish ardor the Americans pursue their own welfare; and to watch the vague dread that constantly torments them lest they should not have chosen the shortest path which may lead to it. A native of the United States clings to this world's goods as if he were certain never to die; and he is

Reprinted from *Democracy in America*, vol. 2, by Alexis de Tocqueville (New York: Colonial Press, 1899).

so hasty in grasping at all within his reach, that one would suppose he was constantly afraid of not living long enough to enjoy them. He clutches everything, he holds nothing fast, but soon loosens his grasp to pursue fresh gratifications.

In the United States a man builds a house to spend his latter years in it, and he sells it before the roof is on: he plants a garden, and lets it just as the trees are coming into bearing: he brings a field into tillage, and leaves other men to gather the crops: he embraces a profession, and gives it up: he settles in a place, which he soon afterwards leaves, to carry his changeable longings elsewhere. If his private affairs leave him any leisure, he instantly plunges into the vortex of politics; and if at the end of a year of unremitting labor he finds he has a few days' vacation, his eager curiosity whirls him over the vast extent of the United States, and he will travel fifteen hundred miles in a few days, to shake off his happiness. Death at length overtakes him, but it is before he is weary of his bootless chase of that complete felicity which is forever on the wing.

ALWAYS IN A HURRY

At first sight there is something surprising in this strange unrest of so many happy men, restless in the midst of abundance. The spectacle itself is however as old as the world; the novelty is to see a whole people furnish an exemplification of it. Their taste for physical gratifications must be regarded as the original source of that secret inquietude which the actions of the Americans betray, and of that inconstancy of which they afford fresh examples every day. He who has set his heart exclusively upon the pursuit of worldly welfare is always in a hurry, for he has but a limited time at his disposal to reach it, to grasp it, and to enjoy it. The recollection of the brevity of life is a constant spur to him. Besides the good things which he possesses, he every instant fancies a thousand others which death will prevent him from trying if he does not try them soon. This thought fills him with anxiety, fear, and regret, and keeps his mind in ceaseless trepidation, which leads him perpetually to change his plans and his abode. If in addition to the taste for physical well-being a social condition be superadded, in which the laws and customs make no condition permanent, here is a great additional stimulant to this restlessness of temper. Men will then be seen continually to change their track, for fear of missing the shortest cut to happiness. It may readily be conceived that if men, passionately bent upon physical gratifications, desire eagerly, they are also easily discouraged: as their ultimate object is to enjoy, the means to reach that object must be prompt and easy, or the trouble of acquiring the gratification would be greater than the gratification itself. Their prevailing frame of mind then is at once ardent and relaxed, violent and enervated. Death is often less dreaded than perseverance in continuous efforts to one end.

The equality of conditions leads by a still straighter road to several of the effects which I have here described. When all the privileges of birth and fortune are abolished, when all professions are accessible to all, and a man's own energies may place him at the top of any one of them, an easy and unbounded career seems open to his ambition, and he will readily persuade himself that he is born to no vulgar destinies. But this is an erroneous notion, which is corrected by daily experience. The same equality which allows every citizen to conceive these lofty hopes, renders all the citizens less able to realize them: it circumscribes their powers on every side, whilst it gives freer scope to their desires. Not only are they themselves powerless, but they are met at every step by immense obstacles, which they did not at first perceive. They have swept away the privileges of some of their fellow-creatures which stood in their way, but they have opened the door to universal competition: the barrier has changed its shape rather than its position. When men are nearly alike, and all follow the same track, it is very difficult for any one individual to walk quick and cleave a way through the dense throng which surrounds and presses him. This constant strife between the propensities springing from the equality of conditions and the means it supplies to satisfy them, harasses and wearies the mind. . . .

INSANITY IS COMMON

Amongst democratic nations men easily attain a certain equality of conditions: they can never attain the equality they desire. It perpetually retires from before them, yet without hiding itself from their sight, and in retiring draws them on. At every moment they think they are about to grasp it; it escapes at every moment from their hold. They are near enough to see its charms, but too far off to enjoy them; and before they have fully tasted its delights they die. To these causes must be attributed that strange melancholy which oftentimes will haunt the inhabitants of democratic countries in the midst of their abundance, and that disgust at life which sometimes seizes upon them in the midst of calm and easy circumstances. Complaints are made in France that the number of suicides increases; in America suicide is rare, but insanity is said to be more common than anywhere else. These are all different symptoms of the same disease. The Americans do not put an end to their lives, however disquieted they may be, because their religion forbids it; and amongst them materialism may be said hardly to exist, notwithstanding the general passion for physical gratification. The will resists—reason frequently gives way.

In democratic ages enjoyments are more intense than in the ages of aristocracy, and especially the number of those who partake in them is larger: but, on the other hand, it must be admitted that man's hopes and his desires are oftener blasted, the soul is more stricken and perturbed, and care itself more keen.

DE TOCQUEVILLE'S AMERICA

Lester D. Langley

One of the most detailed records of U.S. society in the 1830s was, ironically, written by the French aristocrat Alexis de Tocqueville. Originally in America to study the penal system, de Tocqueville traveled extensively and discovered that the people of the United States were exceptionally committed to liberty, equality, and human freedom—at least for the white majority. As a powerful member of the French ruling class, de Tocqueville's praise helped establish the European viewpoint of America as a land of boundless opportunity. In the following excerpt, Lester D. Langley, research professor of history at the University of Georgia, compares de Tocqueville's America to the struggling democracies in South America and the Caribbean.

I n May 1831, two French aristocrats commenced a ten-month study of the prison system of the United States. The initial result of their sojourn was an 1833 publication on U.S. penitentiaries, but the most memorable contribution of this visit was a two-volume work entitled *Democracy in America*, a social portrait of the young republic written by the only member of this duo Americans remember, Alexis de Tocqueville. Jacksonian America, he wrote, was an egalitarian society, where (except for minorities) people might be rich or poor, but according to *American* standards, which meant that opportunities existed in abundance to be born poor but to die rich. In society as in politics, majoritarian wishes and impulses not only prevailed but dictated the rhythms of national life. Contemporary foreign visitors and

Americans validated his judgments [French economists]. Michel Chevalier, who came to the United States two years after Tocqueville departed, described a country of few paupers and a people generally comfortable with their condition. Even Mrs. Francis Trollope [wife of English novelist Anthony Trollope], whose disdain for public habits punctuated her account of American life, departed with the conviction that people in the United States did not suffer from want of life's necessities. Everywhere one looked, there were examples of rags-to-riches biographies, which included, appropriately, President Andrew Jackson.

Such was the judgment of an astute observer who appeared to be validating American "exceptionalism," the belief that North Americans, in contrast to the revolutionaries of Saint Domingue [Italy] and [South] America, had demonstrated that the authority of law and democratic society were capable of coexisting. In its half-century of existence, the United States had experienced social and political disorder and the persistence of impoverishment and, most damning, had expanded slavery's domain, but it had escaped dictatorship or militarism. As Tocqueville contemplated the society that had taken form in the young republic—from the pervasive democratic habits of daily life in the more settled East to the often raucous town politics of the trans-Appalachian West [Tennessee, Kentucky, and Ohio]—he warned of the "tyranny of the majority," but he conveyed few doubts about America's future.

This was unsurprising, given the persuasive festiveness and celebration of Young America in years when Latin America appeared to be plunging into the long despair of the postcolonial era. North Americans had shorn themselves of imperial rule, created the republic of liberty, and, just as quickly, set out to disprove the philosophers by creating an empire of liberty in the West. They described the Haitian revolution as a threat to slavery as an institution and, in more sweeping denunciations, as a menace to civilization. They applauded Latin American revolutionaries for repudiating monarchy, doubted their capacity to emulate the United States' example, and damned their leaders when they proved unable to fashion lasting political institutions. They had taken the measure of the revolutionary age in the New World and found the Haitian and Spanish struggles wanting in virtually every respect. . . .

RESHAPING NATIONAL VALUES

The political culture that took form in the United States after independence appeared to justify Tocqueville's encomia for its unique capability not to resolve but to mitigate persistent social and class antagonisms. What happened was the displacement of a conservative elite by better organized opportunists who not only wanted to share power but, more important, were determined to reshape the nation's political institutions and values. In the process occurred one of several sea changes in the political culture. The United States shed the European character of its politics. City folk and farmers did not exchange places except in American mythology. Rather, the more settled cosmopolitans of the seaboard now had to recognize the political clout of small-town people and farmers whose newfound prosperity and, more important, whose importance as producers of national wealth were undeniable. [Thomas] Jefferson's [presidency] meant not only the defeat of those conservatives who had persevered in the 1780s and ruled in the 1790s but, more fundamentally, signaled a victory of republican ideology, "so enduring that no politician would again think of defending the old order of an elite leadership and passive citizenry."

In Latin America, as in Europe, the difference in meaning between the "better sort" and "meaner sort" conveyed a belief that the social status of these persons was unchangeable. In the United States, however, these words denoted those who subscribed to the imperative of self-improvement and those who, through want of determination or moral character, had opportunities but refused to better themselves. Such an interpretation required a myth of a yeoman [agricultural] republic to take hold of the national imagination—a republic sustained by faith in the unifying power of a common language and in a democratic society expressed in fervent patriot celebration, the broadening of the suffrage, and a people who believed they were exceptional. "It is difficult to describe the rapacity with which the American rushes forward to secure the immense booty which fortune proffers to him," Tocqueville wrote. "He is goaded onward by a passion more intense than love of life. Before him lies a boundless continent, and he urges onward as if time pressed, and he was afraid of finding no room for his exertions."

CELEBRATING THE REVOLUTION

In defining their distinctiveness, Americans looked as much to their recent past, necessarily sanitized in its retelling, as to the seemingly boundless opportunities that lay in their future. . . . People yearned for a nostalgic celebration of the revolutionary "golden age." Although only four signers of the Declaration of Independence were still living in the early 1820s, the passion for what [statesman] Edward Everett called "our heroic age" swept even isolated communities. Every Fourth of July, aging and decrepit revolutionary veterans, most of them ill-treated by a cause they had served, were trundled out as town icons. Inevitably, with the perceptions of class divisions and, especially, the heightened social expectations of artisans and even ordinary laborers, Independence Day acquired a new meaning for those wishing to dramatize their demands. One toast to independence invoked labor's cause: "The Working men—the legitimate children of '76; their sires left them the legacy of freedom and equality. They are now of age, and are laboring to guarantee the principles of the Revolution.". . .

Unlike Europe's aristocratic society with its hierarchies, the democratic society of America was devoid of permanent classes or immobilized groups of people bound together by economic function or ascribed social status. What one did for a living may have given an indication of one's prospects for material improvement, but it did not determine thought, religion, habits, behavior, or character. Democracy was too powerful a social force, opportunity, too widespread to preserve artificial distinctions in social status. The singular mark of status was money, the reward of "virtue" and "intelligence," which prompted the contemporary social commentator Francis Bowen to declare that wealth was "the only distinction that is recognized among us."

Modern society, as Tocqueville recognized, retained large-scale units that dwarfed the individual—for example, the plantation or the large estate—but the democratic urgency of the age dictated the triumph of the small property-holder, the individual. In this vision, other types of modern institutions—plantation agriculture, industry, the military, or the administrative elites already making their appearance—were threats to a democratic society. . . .

A fluidity of society that persuaded Tocqueville of a general equality of opportunity proved a deceptive measure of an [equal] society, however. The United States lacked . . . a precise class system, but it did possess . . . a multiplicity of class structures that varied among communities and depended on such variables as location, comparative economic development, or size. In such a society, wealth can be inequitably or equitably distributed and status high or low. Tocqueville recognized inequities of wealth, of course, but he was routinely distracted by the existence of so many men on the make. . . .

JACKSONIAN DEMOCRACY

As the sharp ideological divisions of the first quarter-century of U.S. independence weakened in a political climate perhaps inaccurately called the Era of Good Feelings, a new generation of political aspirants began to take advantage of the changes wrought in the creation of new states and the expansion of the electorate. Until the 1820s . . . gentry elites had managed to maintain a firm grip on political power with little more than dutiful acknowledgment of the "people's will." Following a faulty logic that new voters would be grateful and keep them in office, they acquiesced in proposals for white manhood suffrage in the original states (except South Carolina and Rhode Island) and encouraged it in the new states in order to attract settlers. Before they realized what was happening, they were suddenly confronted with a massive electorate more inclined to respond to a leader who could rouse their emotions or appeal to what members of the old order disdainfully called the "mobocracy."

In the spirit of an . . . egalitarian age, political ideology, once a great debate between learned men over the nature of government, had as much to do with character, personality, and the ability to attract a following. [Andrew] Jackson was the symbol of the age. When he left office in 1837, turning over the presidency to the country's first "party politician," Martin Van Buren, even Whig opponents who had railed against Jackson's tyrannical use of power and blatant appeal to the masses had begun to imitate his political style in electioneering. They knew well enough that the most dramatic expansion in the electorate had occurred among white males of modest means and that the surest means of keeping government out of the hands of the vaunted common man lay in creating political machines for control at the local level and political parties at the state and national level dominated by men of means. "There never was a period in the history of our country," wrote a westerner, "in which its public men have sought popularity, power, and office with so much avidity . . . [and] display a dissoluteness altogether incompatible with the genius of a sober-minded people.

WORLD HISTORY BY ERA

1838–1848

CHAPTER 6

THE MANIFEST DESTINY OF THE UNITED STATES

JOHN L. O'SULLIVAN

The term *manifest destiny* was first used in 1845 by John L. O'Sullivan, the editor of the *Democratic Review*. In the flowery language of the mid-nineteenth century, O'Sullivan claimed that it was the heavenly fate of the United States, as preordained by God, to take control of all of the lands on the American continent, from the Atlantic to the Pacific Oceans, regardless of the fact that they were inhabited by Native Americans, and were also claimed, in part, by Great Britain and Mexico. The concept gained widespread acceptance and was later used to justify the territorial ambitions of the United States in lands around the globe.

The American people having derived their origin from many other nations, and the Declaration of National Independence being entirely based on the great principle of human equality, these facts demonstrate at once our disconnected position as regards any other nation; that we have, in reality, but little connection with the past history of any of them, and still less with all antiquity, its glories, or its crimes. On the contrary, our national birth was the beginning of a new history, the formation and progress of an untried political system, which separates us from the past and connects us with the future only; and so far as regards the entire development of the natural rights of man, in moral, political, and national life, we may confidently assume that our country is destined to be *the great nation* of futurity. . . .

Excerpted from "The Great Nation of Futurity," by John L. O'Sullivan, *United States Magazine and Democratic Review*, vol. 6 (November 1839), pp. 426–30.

How many nations have had their decline and fall, because the equal rights of the minority were trampled on by the despotism of the majority; or the interests of the many sacrificed to the aristocracy of the few; or the rights and interests of all given up to the monarchy of one? . . .

What friend of human liberty, civilization, and refinement, can cast his view over the past history of the monarchies and aristocracies of antiquity, and not deplore that they ever existed? What philanthropist can contemplate the oppressions, the cruelties, and injustice inflicted by them on the masses of mankind, and not turn with moral horror from the retrospect?

America is destined for better deeds. It is our unparalleled glory that we have no reminiscences of battle fields, but in defence of humanity, of the oppressed of all nations, of the rights of conscience, the rights of personal enfranchisement. Our annals describe no scenes of horrid carnage, where men were led on by hundreds of thousands to slay one another, dupes and victims to emperors, kings, nobles, demons in the human form called heroes. We have had patriots to defend our homes, our liberties, but no aspirants to crowns or thrones; nor have the American people ever suffered themselves to be led on by wicked ambition to depopulate the land, to spread desolation far and wide, that a human being might be placed on a seat of supremacy.

A NATION OF HUMAN PROGRESS

We have no interest in the scenes of antiquity, only as lessons of avoidance of nearly all their examples. The expansive future is our arena, and for our history. We are entering on its untrodden space, with the truths of God in our minds, beneficent objects in our hearts, and with a clear conscience unsullied by the past. We are the nation of human progress, and who will, what can, set limits to our onward march? Providence is with us, and no earthly power can. We point to the everlasting truth on the first page of our national declaration, and we proclaim to the millions of other lands, that "the gates of hell"—the powers of aristocracy and monarchy—"shall not prevail against it."

The far-reaching, the boundless future will be the era of American greatness. In its magnificent domain of space and time, the nation of many nations is destined to manifest to mankind the excellence of divine principles; to establish on earth the noblest temple ever dedicated to the worship of the Most High—the Sacred and the True. Its floor shall be a hemisphere—its roof the firmament of the star-studded heavens, and its congregation a Union of many Republics, comprising hundreds of happy millions, calling, owning no man master, but governed by God's natural and moral law of equality, the law of brotherhood—of "peace and good will amongst men.". . .

Yes, we are the nation of progress, of individual freedom, of universal enfranchisement. . . . We must onward to the fulfilment of our mission—to the entire development of the principle of our organization—freedom of conscience, freedom of person, freedom of trade and business pursuits, universality of freedom and equality. This is our high destiny, and in nature's eternal, inevitable decree of cause and effect we must accomplish it. All this will be our future history, to establish on earth the moral dignity and salvation of man—the immutable truth and beneficence of God. For this blessed mission to the nations of the world, which are shut out from the life-giving light of truth, has America been chosen; and her high example shall smite unto death the tyranny of kings, hierarchs, and oligarchs, and carry the glad tidings of peace and good will where myriads now endure an existence scarcely more enviable than that of beasts of the field. Who, then, can doubt that our country is destined to be *the great nation* of futurity?

THE EUROPEAN REVOLUTIONS OF 1848

PAUL D. LENSINK

In 1848 a wave of revolutionary fervor swept across Europe as poor and middle-class citizens attempted to gain voting rights, access to education, shorter working hours, and better pay for their labors. The revolutions of 1848 occurred in nearly every European country, including France, Italy, Prussia, Austria, Germany, and Russia. All of these uprisings were quickly defeated by authoritarian monarchs who instituted censorship, mass arrests, and other tools of oppression. Fulbright scholar and historian Paul D. Lensink explores the failed revolutions of 1848 and their long-term consequences for the governments and people of Europe.

The year 1848 was unique in European history. Never before had the revolutionary current been so strong. In all, some fifty separate revolts and uprisings took place, and many of these were amazingly successful. Within the space of a few weeks, revolutionary forces had succeeded in toppling several governments. Remarkably, these revolutions took place in an area marked by great geographic, social, political, and economic diversity. Some regions in western Europe were more economically and socially advanced, while large areas in southern and eastern Europe remained backward. Political systems under attack ranged from a constitutional monarchy in France to the absolutist multinational empire of the Habsburgs [dynasty in Austria]. The revolutionaries themselves had different motives and often pursued contradictory aims. Nationalism galvanized some of the revolutions, while economic hardship and political alienation sustained others. The bourgeoisie wanted to ensure property and voting rights, while urban workers demanded job security and food. Peasants, who formed the vast majority of Europe's population, demanded an end to serfdom, the legal system which made them virtual slaves to the landlords.

Because of the diverse nature of the Revolutions of 1848, assessing their significance is a complex task. No general interpretation can explain each case, or even the whole revolutionary episode. Each of the revolutions took place under particular national and local circumstances. Nonetheless, the revolutions did share more than the time frame in which they occurred. The impact of the revolutions spread well beyond the particulars of each situation. Some common conditions and attitudes had to prevail for the revolutionary current to spread so quickly across national boundaries. While it is important to remember that none of the revolutions was exactly alike, the best way to determine their overall historical significance is to identify some of their fundamental characteristics and consequences.

FAILED STRUGGLES

One of the most obvious features of the revolutions was that they all eventually shared the same fate: failure. By the summer of 1848, most of the revolts had lost momentum as the revolutionaries began to experience serious differences over methods and aims. This allowed the antirevolutionary forces time to regroup and to gain strength. By 1849 only the Hungarians and Venetians held out against the conservative [antirevolutionary] reaction sweeping across Europe. Then in August, the Habsburg army, with some outside help from the Russians, defeated these revolutions as well. Although the Revolutions of 1848 started with great promise, no revolutionary regime was able to maintain power. Most of the European aristocracy preserved its entrenched position at the top of society, and, with the exception of France, the pre-1848 governments regained power and reestablished authoritarian rule. Even many moderate liberals sided with the conservative elements of society because of the threat of social revolution posed by the lower classes. The conservatives seemed to become even more unified and powerful in the wake of the defeated revolutions.

In France, after the socialist revolutionaries were crushed . . . , the Constituent Assembly passed a constitution that called for a strong presidency. In December, Louis Napoleon, the nephew of Napoleon Bonaparte, won the election for president by an overwhelming majority, thereby inaugurating the so-called French Second Republic. Louis Napoleon was to have a four-year term.

However, the new president, dissatisfied with this limit on his rule, illegally dismissed the assembly in 1851 and took power in a coup d'état. He then called an election which extended his presidency to a ten-year term. There was some resistance to this move, but protests were crushed by the army. The following year Louis Napoleon held another plebiscite which named him hereditary emperor. Louis Napoleon, now Napoleon III, replaced the Second Republic with his own personal dictatorship. Although his rule was ratified by popular vote, the government was basically authoritarian and composed mainly of men of the old order. This appeared to be a resounding defeat for the ideals of the 1848 revolution in France.

In the German states, the liberals in the Frankfurt Assembly had failed to create a unified Germany. Although the assembly elected Frederick William emperor of the new German state, the Prussian king refused the throne, not wishing to accept a crown offered by an elected parliament. This proved to be a major defeat for liberalism in Germany. In 1849 Frederick William disbanded Prussia's Constituent Assembly. He granted a basically conservative constitution that allowed conservatives to maintain control over a weak parliament. . . .

The Habsburg Empire became even more centralized and reactionary than it had been prior to the revolutions. The government in Vienna returned to the system created by the archconservative [prince Klemens von] Metternich and strengthened it even further. In 1851, the government repealed the constitution passed in 1848 and canceled the list of rights granted in 1849. New laws abolished elected councils at virtually all levels, even those that had existed prior to 1848, and created a new, highly centralized administration. The laws also introduced Austrian law into the Hungarian lands of the empire and assured a superior position to German-speaking subjects. There were virtually no institutions left to check the power of the central authorities. For several years Vienna ruled the empire as a kind of conquered territory.

The conservative reaction was also strong in various Italian states. The regime in Modena jailed liberals and closed universities. Pope Pius IX became an opponent of both liberalism and nationalism, and denounced the war against Catholic Austria. In Naples, the government worked with organized crime in order to strengthen its authority. Only in the kingdom of Piedmont did the government maintain the liberal constitution passed in 1848.

In the short term, the 1848 revolutions, or rather their defeat, led to strengthened authoritarianism. Government authorities and police censored potentially revolutionary publications, arrested political opponents, and, in general, created a climate of repression. The power of the military also expanded in most of the countries that had experienced revolution. The French revolutionary Pierre-Joseph Proudhon lamented, "We have been beaten and humiliated. We have been scattered, imprisoned, disarmed, and gagged. The fate of European democracy has slipped from our hands—from the hands of the people—into those of the Praetorian Guard."

Because of the defeat of the revolutions, many of the problems that had caused the upheaval in the first place were not immediately addressed. The urban poor still endured the misery of filthy living conditions, and workers did not gain greater access to education or shorter hours. Artisans still faced the prospect of losing their livelihood because of industrialization. The middle classes did not establish a lasting government enshrining liberal values, though in many cases they did gain expanded voting rights. On the surface, it appeared that many average Europeans became politically apathetic, having lost hope for meaningful change.

Many observers have considered the Revolutions of 1848 an episode that might have advanced ideas such as liberalism and democracy. History seemed to be progressing in that direction. The political philosophy of liberalism had spread with the success of the French Revolution and the conquests of Napoleon. The revolutions in the first half of the nineteenth century suggested that it was only a matter of time until governments based on liberal values replaced the conservative monarchies. At first, it seemed that the revolutions in 1848 might accomplish just that. This made their ultimate failure all the more disappointing. The conservative reaction that ensued made the defeat of the revolutions appear even more complete. The famous British historian G.M. Trevelyan even asserted, "1848 was the turning point at which modern history failed to turn." The revolutions should have been the point at which the old regime was finally and completely overthrown, but this was far from the case. Some historians have argued that the revolutions were not really revolutions at all, for they did not succeed in advancing a new political system or structure. . . .

TRANSFORMING EUROPE

It is necessary to look beyond the immediate political aftermath of the revolutions. Even though conservatives managed to regain and even to consolidate power, they had to operate under a new set of realities. Revolution had proved capable of spreading quickly, and although the revolutionaries were defeated in 1848, the ideas brought to the forefront during the unrest could not easily be swept away. Concepts like nationalism and universal suffrage were now an undeniable part of political life. The conservatives could not simply turn back to pre-1848 policies; they had to develop new and more effective ways to meet the challenge of revolutionary ideas. Ironically, the same authoritarian leaders who crushed the revolutions eventually came to institute many of the ideas first brought to the forefront during the upheaval of 1848. Though defeated in the short run, the revolutions unleashed ideas that became a natural part of political and social life in the ensuing decades. In this way the revolutions helped transform Europe.

Although conservatives returned to power after the 1848 revolutions, people no longer simply accepted monarchy as the natural order of politics and society. The traditional system of the old regime had lost its authority. Very few leaders could hope to survive as champions only of absolutism and reactionary politics. As the post-1848 leaders came to terms with this fact, they began to see that they would have to pursue new policies to reinforce their power. They had to learn the politics of the people. Even conservative leaders began to talk about influencing public opinion, and they adopted strategies to integrate discontented social groups into the existing political systems. Because they were still fearful of revolution, conservatives recognized the need to provide some outlet for political and social dissent. Thus, in many cases, the post-1848 regimes granted limited political rights and created some form of democratic institutions. However, conservatives generally maintained control of the political process through skillful manipulation of the voters and the political institutions. Ultimately, the authoritarian governments that emerged in the aftermath of 1848 proved quite different than their predecessors.

Examples of the new authoritarian tactics can be found in several of the major states that experienced revolution in 1848. In France, Napoleon III became a masterful manipulator of popular politics. He was sensitive to public opinion and tried to foster popular support for his policies. He reintroduced universal male suffrage and repeatedly tested his right to rule by calling elections. Parliament also remained intact, though it had little say in important government matters. The French emperor helped build economic prosperity by promoting public works projects and creating new investment banks. Napoleon III was one of the first modern leaders to rule not simply by force or claim to divine right, but by propaganda and populist appeal that could be managed well by a capable authoritarian.

Prussia also made steps toward a modern political structure, even though conservatives retained control over the governing process. The parliament, though weak, proved to be an important feature of politics since it provided an outlet for dissenting viewpoints. The Prussian government also made decisions to appeal to large segments of the population. The peasantry benefited from the abolition of serfdom and the limited redistribution of land. At the same time, these reforms did not greatly threaten the interests of the landowning class. The middle classes also made important gains as the Prussian government started to promote industrial development and economic growth, and reformed the bureaucracy and judicial system. These policies helped Prussia out of the stagnation that had contributed to the revolution in 1848. Certainly not all problems were solved, but there was enough progress so that most segments of society no longer favored revolution as a solution.

In the Habsburg lands, the Revolutions of 1848 demonstrated that nationalism had the potential to rip the multinational empire apart. If the Habsburg monarchy was to survive, its leaders had to do more than simply revert to traditional policies. Consequently, the Habsburg government began to modernize and reform the empire's antiquated administrative structure. Emperor Francis Joseph issued laws intended to make government more efficient and effective. They reformed the civil service, standardized the tax system and commercial laws, and encouraged economic development. Francis Joseph also maintained one important change made during the revolutions, the abolition of serfdom. This met the most basic demand of the peasantry. Even under the most authoritarian systems, leaders had to come to terms with a political environment altered by the revolutions.

GIVING VOICE TO THE PEOPLE

The events of 1848 enabled many Europeans who had previously had little political experience to participate in the political problems of the day. Those who usually had little say in politics and society, such as women, workers, and artisans, provided the muscle for revolutionary demonstrations. People came to believe that politics had relevance for their daily lives and that they could gain better living conditions. "All change!" was a common slogan of the revolutions. Ideas that had once been discussed only by liberal-minded intellectuals became open to many more people. The concepts of nationalism, democracy, and equality supplied powerful motivation for large segments of the population. Although the defeat of the revolutions caused some people to withdraw from political involvement, the experience gained during 1848 generated a loyalty to certain political ideas. Such ideological commitments survived to resurface in better times.

The revolutions also revealed the social division and new class structure that was emerging in Europe. One of the primary reasons the revolutions failed was the lack of unity among the revolutionary elements of society. In most cases the revolutions actually began as mass protest movements of the urban poor. Workers and artisans fought most of the street battles and manned the barricades. At first the real revolutions had no leaders. Rather, the lower classes actually pushed politically aware intellectuals who also favored change to participate in the revolution. Although intellectuals, workers, peasants, and others found a common cause in making revolution, this did not provide a basis for lasting political cooperation. When the time came to form new governments and make reforms, the different groups promoting revolution split apart. Advocates of liberalism, many of whom came from the bourgeoisie, hoped to consolidate their own positions by assuring property rights and limited political democracy. The lower classes, especially poorer urban workers, wanted real equal rights, social justice, and secure employment. For these people liberalism did not go far enough; they wanted social revolution. The attitude of the lower classes and the prospect of more violent agitation worried liberals. While they wanted some reforms, they could not go along with social and political change that would threaten stability and social order.

In the end, liberals proved more willing to acquiesce in a return to conservative control than to accept social revolution. They were unwilling to battle openly against the established order. Hence, liberals withdrew from the revolutions and made it possible for dedicated conservatives to reassert authority. The revolutions failed not because the conservatives defeated progressive forces, but because those classes of society with some power and wealth, including most liberals, favored order over true social revolution.

As a result of this split, the revolutions served to promote a new kind of class antagonism. The lower classes found that they could not count on liberal intellectuals and the bourgeoisie for support. The lack of revolutionary solidarity demonstrated that simply overthrowing the old order was not enough to achieve real change. The resulting disillusion convinced many workers that socialism and class solidarity were the only answer. This created a basis for the radical socialism advocated by Karl Marx and Friedrich Engels, two German political theorists. The men first outlined their socialist ideas in the *Communist Manifesto* (1848), which asserted that class conflict was inevitable and that workers, if they wanted real power, would have to overthrow the bourgeoisie in a violent revolution. The conflicting goals and aspirations of different classes revealed in 1848 remained an important feature of politics in the second half of the nineteenth century. Nineteenth-century liberals and socialists continued to disagree greatly in their views on the role of government and the classes of society.

A NEW NATIONALISM

The power of nationalism also proved to be one of the most important legacies of the 1848 revolutions. Prior to 1848, nationalism was largely the purview of intellectuals, who were primarily interested in cultural aspects of nationalism such as literature, history, and language. However, the 1848 revolutions demonstrated that nationalism could have broad political appeal and provide a rationale for changing government. Many liberal revolutionaries argued that sovereignty should rest with the people of the nation, not with a monarchy. In the German- and Italian-speaking lands, these revolutionaries advocated national unification as a way to make political change. Both Germans and Italians had long been separated into different states and principalities, and many revolutionaries hoped that a constitutional government could be created for a unified state.

Although neither Italy nor Germany was unified in 1848, nationalism and national unification did become more acceptable notions. Just as with some other political ideas, the authoritarian leaders realized that nationalism was a force they could manipulate for their own purposes. It provided ready justification for strengthening central control and military power. It could also help to reconcile class conflicts within the state. . . .

In the multinational Habsburg Empire, nationalism played a divisive rather than a unifying role. During the 1848 revolutions, self-determination first became a concrete goal for many of the nationalities in the Habsburg lands. The revolutions also awakened national feeling among the empire's Slavic population, including Czechs, Slovaks, Croats, Slovenes, and Serbs. Slavic intellectuals held a congress in Prague in 1848. The participants in the Slav Congress advocated ethnic and linguistic unity as a way to defend against German nationalism, and some even called for an independent Slavic state in Europe. Nationalism was also the primary cause for the Hungarian revolution, which was successful in large part because the disparate classes in Hungary joined forces against the imperial authorities. Unfortunately, nationalism frequently was transformed into chauvinism when people became prejudiced against other nationalities. Hungarians, for example, wanted national independence for themselves, but they were not willing to grant the same rights to national minorities living in Hungarian-controlled lands.

Although the Habsburg government managed to quash national aspirations for a time, it could not do so indefinitely. The government passed reforms to improve the bureaucracy, but this did little to solve the empire's nationality conflicts. To the contrary, some of the new policies actually made the nationality problem worse. For example, the reformed civil service was overwhelmingly German, and this antagonized much of the empire's non-German population. The Hungarians, who had the most success fighting for independence in 1848–1849, finally gained autonomy through an agreement called the Compromise of 1867, which gave the Hungarians control over their domestic affairs, but preserved a unified imperial army and ministry of foreign affairs. This satisfied the Hungarians for a time, but the other nationalities in the Hungarian lands, such as Slovaks and Croats, chafed under Hungarian control and continued to aspire to autonomy for their own nations.

The realization of nationalist goals in the decades after 1848 prompted a significant shift in the European balance of power. As a unified nation, Germany became stronger and exerted much more influence in European politics. Unified Italy also entered the ranks of the Great Powers. Napoleon III, the new emperor of France, deliberately cultivated French nationalism as he sought to restore France to the position of grandeur and power that it had lost in 1815. Meanwhile, the Habsburg Empire became weaker as nationalism continued to threaten its stability and integrity. The 1848 revolutions, by legitimating and encouraging national aspirations, helped to change the international power structure of Europe.

The economic consequences of the revolutions are more difficult to determine. There was unprecedented economic growth in Europe in the two decades after 1848, but it would be inaccurate to portray this wholly as a result of the revolutions. It can be said, however, that the revolutions did promote some changes that certainly facilitated economic growth. The breakdown of old customs and the spread of new ideas encouraged people to move from their traditional activities and environment. The abolition of feudal restrictions made it possible for peasants to migrate to cities and to work in factories. The fear of revolution also led many post-1848 regimes to modernize their administration. Governments promoted economic growth by establishing uniform laws and lowering trade barriers. In general, the middle class made the most significant economic gains after 1848. It benefited greatly from economic expansion, and greater wealth ultimately led to more influence in politics.

THE END OF THE REVOLUTIONARY ERA

Despite its failure to establish new political structures, the mid-century upheaval represents a pivotal point in the history of nineteenth-century Europe. For nearly sixty years, since the French Revolution in 1789, Europe had experienced recurrent revolts and revolutions. However, this "age of revolutions" came to an end with the Revolutions of 1848. After them, there were no significant revolutions in Europe except under the stress of war. Yet many of the goals of the revolutionaries were met in more gradual ways. People no longer accepted traditional notions of politics such as aristocratic privilege and divinely appointed dynasties. Authoritarian governments learned to offset potential unrest by granting limited concessions to certain groups in society. Hence, the very leaders who defeated the revolutions later helped to advance many revolutionary ideas.

The year 1848 also marks the opening of an era. The issues and goals raised by the revolutions, although not met at the time, later spread and became a common part of the political and social order. Socialism, political democracy, liberalism, and nationalism all promoted the development of a modern political consciousness. Change could be achieved more gradually because the state became more organized, prosperity expanded, and the middle classes renounced revolution. Peasants also were less likely to support revolution since governments granted their primary demand, an end to serfdom. The lower classes developed a political sense which in time gave them a stronger voice to demand reforms. Workers began to form unions, and universal suffrage became more common and accepted. The year 1848 became known as the "springtime of peoples," and many nationalities looked to 1848 as the moment of national awakening. The changes did not occur immediately, but the revolutions did pave the way for the transition from a feudal society to an industrial society with a modern state structure. In this sense, the 1848 revolutions did change the world, though not as quickly as the revolutionaries would have liked.

THE INDUSTRIAL REVOLUTION'S EFFECT ON WORKERS

FRIEDRICH ENGELS

Friedrich Engels was the son of a German manufacturer who ran a factory in Manchester, England, before becoming an advocate for the Communist political system with his associate Karl Marx. In the following excerpt, written in 1845, Engels details the history of the Industrial Revolution in England and its negative effect on formerly independent weavers and spinners.

T he history of the proletariat in England begins with the second half of the last century, with the invention of the steam-engine and of machinery for working cotton. These inventions gave rise . . . to an industrial revolution, a revolution which altered the whole civil society; one, the historical importance of which is only now beginning to be recognised. England is the classic soil of this transformation, . . . and England is, therefore, the classic land of its chief product also, the proletariat. Only in England can the proletariat be studied in all its relations and from all sides. . . .

Before the introduction of machinery, the spinning and weaving of raw materials was carried on in the working-man's home. Wife and daughter spun the yarn that the father wove or that they sold, if he did not work it up himself. These weaver families lived in the country in the neighbourhood of the towns, and could get on fairly well with their wages, because the home market was almost the only one, and the crushing power of compe-

Excerpted from *The Condition of the Working Class in England in 1844*, by Friedrich Engels, translated by F.K. Wischnewetzky, London 1892.

tition that came later, with the conquest of foreign markets and the extension of trade, did not yet press upon wages. There was, further, a constant increase in the demand for the home market, keeping pace with the slow increase in population and employing all the workers; and there was also the impossibility of vigorous competition of the workers among themselves, consequent upon the rural dispersion of their homes. So it was that the weaver was usually in a position to lay by something, and rent a little piece of land, that he cultivated in his leisure hours, of which he had as many as he chose to take, since he could weave whenever and as long as he pleased. True, he was a bad farmer and managed his land inefficiently, often obtaining but poor crops; nevertheless, he was no proletarian, he had a stake in the country, he was permanently settled, and stood one step higher in society than the English workman of to-day.

So the workers vegetated throughout a passably comfortable existence, leading a righteous and peaceful life in all piety and probity; and their material position was far better than that of their successors. They did not need to overwork; they did no more than they chose to do, and yet earned what they needed. They had leisure for healthful work in garden or field, work which, in itself, was recreation for them, and they could take part besides in the recreations and games of their neighbours, and all these games—bowling, cricket, football, etc., contributed to their physical health and vigour. . . . Their children grew up in the fresh country air, and, if they could help their parents at work, it was only occasionally. . . .

CHANGES IN PRODUCTION

The first invention which gave rise to a radical change in the state of the English workers was the jenny, invented in the year 1764 by a weaver, James Hargreaves of Standhill, near Blackburn, in North Lancashire. This machine was the rough beginning of the later invented [spinning] mule, and was moved by hand. Instead of one spindle like the ordinary spinning-wheel, it carried sixteen or eighteen manipulated by a single workman. This invention made it possible to deliver more yarn than heretofore. . . . The demand for woven goods, already increasing, rose yet more in consequence of the cheapness of these goods, which cheapness, in turn, was the outcome of the diminished cost of producing the yarn. More weavers were needed, and weavers' wages rose. Now that the weaver could earn more at his loom, he gradually abandoned his farming, and gave his whole time to weaving. . . . By degrees the class of farming weavers wholly disappeared, and was merged in the newly arising class of weavers who lived

wholly upon wages, had no property whatever, not even the pre-
tended property of a holding, and so became working-men, proletarians. Moreover, the old relation between spinner and weaver
was destroyed. Hitherto, so far as this had been possible, yarn had
been spun and woven under one roof. Now that the jenny as well
as the loom required a strong hand, men began to spin, and whole
families lived by spinning, while others laid the antiquated, superseded spinning-wheel aside; and, if they had not means of
purchasing a jenny, were forced to live upon the wages of the father alone. Thus began with spinning and weaving that division
of labour which has since been so infinitely perfected. . . .

MACHINE-WORK OVER HAND-WORK

Meanwhile, the industrial movement did not stop here. Single
capitalists began to set up spinning jennies in great buildings and
to use water-power for driving them, so placing themselves in a
position to diminish the number of workers, and sell their yarn
more cheaply than single spinners could do who moved their
own machines by hand. There were constant improvements in the
jenny, so that machines continually became antiquated, and must
be altered or even laid aside; and though the capitalists could hold
out by the application of water-power even with the old machinery, for the single spinner this was impossible. And the factory
system, the beginning of which was thus made, received a fresh
extension in 1767, through the [wool] spinning throstle invented
by Richard Arkwright, a barber. . . . After the steam-engine, this
is the most important mechanical invention of the 18th century. It
was calculated from the beginning for mechanical motive power,
and was based upon wholly new principles. By the combination
of the . . . jenny and throstle, Samuel Crompton . . . contrived the
mule in 1785, and as Arkwright invented the carding engine, and
preparatory . . . frames about the same time, the factory system
became the prevailing one for the spinning of cotton. By means
of trifling modifications these machines were gradually adapted
to the spinning of flax, and so to the superseding of hand-work
here, too. But even then, the end was not yet. In the closing years
of the last century, Dr. Cartwright, a country parson, had invented
the power-loom, and about 1804 had so far perfected it, that it
could successfully compete with the hand-weaver; and all this
machinery was made doubly important by James Watt's steam-
engine, invented in 1764, and used for supplying motive power
for spinning since 1785.

With these inventions, since improved from year to year, the
victory of machine-work over hand-work in the chief branches
of English industry was won; and the history of the latter from

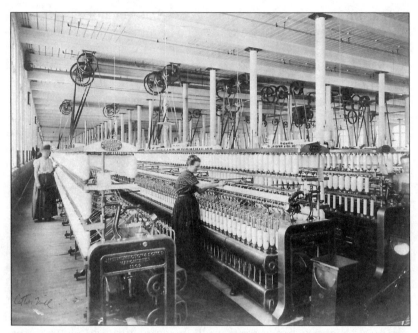

The Industrial Revolution had a dramatic impact on textile workers' lives—taking them away from their homes and families and forcing them to work in the factories.

that time forward simply relates how the hand-workers have been driven by machinery from one position after another. The consequences of this were, on the one hand, a rapid fall in price of all manufactured commodities, prosperity of commerce and manufacture, the conquest of nearly all the unprotected foreign markets, the sudden multiplication of capital and national wealth; on the other hand, a still more rapid multiplication of the proletariat, the destruction of all property-holding and of all security of employment for the working-class, demoralisation, political excitement, and all those facts so highly repugnant to Englishmen in comfortable circumstances, which we shall have to consider in the following pages. Having already seen what a transformation in the social condition of the lower classes a single such clumsy machine as the jenny had wrought, there is no cause for surprise as to that which a complete and interdependent system of finely adjusted machinery has brought about, machinery which receives raw material and turns out woven goods. . . .

Such, in brief, is the history of English industrial development in the past sixty years, a history which has no counterpart in the annals of humanity. Sixty, eighty years ago, England was a country like every other, with small towns, few and simple industries, and a thin but *proportionally* large agricultural population. To-day it is a country like *no* other, with a capital of two and a half million inhabitants; with vast manufacturing cities; with an industry that supplies the world, and produces almost everything by means of the most complex machinery; with an industrious, intelligent, dense population, of which two-thirds are employed in trade and commerce, and composed of classes wholly different; forming, in fact, with other customs and other needs, a different nation from the England of those days. The industrial revolution is of the same importance for England as the political revolution for France, and the philosophical revolution for Germany; and the difference between England in 1760 and in 1844 is at least as great as that between France, under the [monarchy] and during the revolution. . . . But the mightiest result of this industrial transformation is the English proletariat.

We have already seen how the proletariat was called into existence by the introduction of machinery. The rapid extension of manufacture demanded hands, wages rose, and troops of workmen migrated from the agricultural districts to the towns. Population multiplied enormously, and nearly all the increase took place in the proletariat. Further, Ireland had entered upon an orderly development only since the beginning of the eighteenth century. There, too, the population, more than decimated by English cruelty in earlier disturbances, now rapidly multiplied, especially after the advance in manufacture began to draw masses of Irishmen towards England. Thus arose the great manufacturing and commercial cities of the British Empire, in which at least three-fourths of the population belong to the working-class, while the lower middle-class consists only of small shopkeepers, and very very few handicraftsmen. For, though the rising manufacture first attained importance by transforming tools into machines, workrooms into factories, and consequently, the toiling lower middle-class into the toiling proletariat, and the former large merchants into manufacturers, though the lower middle-class was thus early crushed out, and the population reduced to the two opposing elements, workers and capitalists, this happened outside of the domain of manufacture proper, in the province of handicraft and retail trade as well. In the place of the former masters and apprentices, came great capitalists and working-men who had no prospect of rising above their class. Hand-work was carried on after the fashion of factory work, the division of labour was strictly applied, and small employers who could not compete with great establishments were forced down into the proletariat. At the same time the destruction of the former organisation of hand-work, and the disappearance of the lower middle-class deprived the working-man of all possibility of rising into the middle-class himself. Hitherto he had always had the prospect of establishing himself somewhere as masters [artisan], perhaps employing journeymen and apprentices; but now, when master [artisans] were crowded out by manufacturers, when large capital had become necessary for carrying on work independently, the working-class became, for the first time, an integral, permanent class of the population, whereas it had formerly often been merely a transition leading to the bourgeoisie. Now, he who was born to toil had no other prospect than that of remaining a toiler all his life. Now, for the first time, therefore, the proletariat was in a position to undertake an independent movement. . . .

Hence . . . the deep wrath of the whole working-class, from Glasgow to London, against the rich, by whom they are systematically plundered and mercilessly left to their fate, a wrath which before too long a time goes by, a time almost within the power of man to predict, must break out into a Revolution in comparison with which the French Revolution, and the year 1794, will prove to have been child's play.

THE *COMMUNIST* *MANIFESTO*

KARL MARX AND FRIEDRICH ENGELS

Inspired by the revolutions of 1848, German economist, philosopher, and revolutionary Karl Marx wrote the *Communist Manifesto* with a wealthy English manufacturer named Friedrich Engels. The short pamphlet was intended to act as a political platform for the small international workers' party known as the Communist League. The authors claimed that all history was a result of class struggles between working people, known as the proletariat, and business owners, or the bourgeoisie. In the following excerpt, Marx and Engels discuss their reasons for wanting to unite the proletariat into a workers' party while confiscating the private property of the bourgeoisie.

I n what relation do the Communists stand to the proletarians as a whole?
   The Communists do not form a separate party opposed to other working class parties.
   They have no interests separate and apart from those of the proletariat as a whole.
   They do not set up any sectarian principles of their own by which to shape and mould the proletarian movement.
   The Communists are distinguished from the other working class parties by this only: 1. In the national struggles of the proletarians of the different countries they point out and bring to the front the common interests of the entire proletariat, independently of all nationality; 2, In the various stages of development which the struggle of the working class against the bourgeoisie

Excerpted from *Manifesto of the Communist Party*, by Karl Marx and Friedrich Engels, translated by Samuel Moore (Chicago: Encyclopaedia Britannica, 1952).

has to pass through they always and everywhere represent the interests of the movement as a whole.

The Communists, therefore, are on the one hand, practically, the most advanced and resolute section of the working class parties of every country, that section which pushes forward all others; on the other hand, theoretically, they have over the great mass of the proletariat the advantage of clearly understanding the line of march, the conditions, and the ultimate general results of the proletarian movement.

The immediate aim of the Communists is the same as that of all the other proletarian parties: formation of the proletariat into a class, overthrow of bourgeois supremacy, conquest of political power by the proletariat.

The theoretical conclusions of the Communists are in no way based on ideas or principles that have been invented or discovered by this or that would-be universal reformer.

They merely express in general terms actual relations springing from an existing class struggle, from a historical movement going on under our very eyes. The abolition of existing property relations is not at all a distinctive feature of Communism.

All property relations in the past have continually been subject to historical change consequent upon the change in historical conditions.

The French Revolution, for example, abolished feudal property in favour of bourgeois property.

The distinguishing feature of Communism is not the abolition of property generally, but the abolition of bourgeois property. But modern bourgeois private property is the final and most complete expression of the system of producing and appropriating products that is based on class antagonisms, on the exploitation of the many by the few.

In this sense the theory of the Communists may be summed up in the single sentence: abolition of private property.

We Communists have been reproached with the desire of abolishing the right of personally acquiring property as the fruit of a man's own labour, which property is alleged to be the groundwork of all personal freedom, activity and independence.

Hard-won, self-acquired, self-earned property! Do you mean the property of the petty artisan and of the small peasant, a form of property that preceded the bourgeois form? There is no need to abolish that; the development of industry has to a great extent already destroyed it and is still destroying it daily. . . .

Let us now take wage labour.

The average price of wage labour is the minimum wage, i.e., . . . the means of subsistence which is absolutely requisite to keep the labourer in bare existence as a labourer. What, therefore, the wage labourer appropriates by means of his labour merely suffices to prolong and reproduce a bare existence. We by no means intend to abolish this personal appropriation of the products of labour, an appropriation that is made for the maintenance and repro-duction of human life and that leaves no surplus wherewith to command the labour of others. All that we want to do away with is the miserable character of this appropriation, under which the labourer lives merely to increase capital, and is allowed to live only insofar as the interest of the ruling class requires it.

In bourgeois society living labour is but a means to increase accumulated labour. In Communist society accumulated labour is but a means to widen, to enrich, to promote the existence of the labourer.

In bourgeois society, therefore, the past dominates the present; in Communist society, the present dominates the past. In bour-geois society capital is independent and has individuality, while the living person is dependent and has no individuality.

And the abolition of this state of things is called by the bour-geois, abolition of individuality and freedom! And rightly so. The abolition of bourgeois individuality, bourgeois independence, and bourgeois freedom is undoubtedly aimed at.

By freedom is meant, under the present bourgeois conditions of production, free trade, free selling and buying.

But if selling and buying disappears, free selling and buying disappears also. This talk about free selling and buying, and all the other "brave words" of our bourgeoisie about freedom in general, have a meaning, if any, only in contrast with restricted selling and buying, with the fettered traders of the Middle Ages, but have no meaning when opposed to the Communist abolition of buying and selling, of the bourgeois conditions of production, and of the bourgeoisie itself.

You are horrified at our intending to do away with private property. But in your existing society private property is already done away with for nine-tenths of the population; its existence for the few is solely due to its non-existence in the hands of those nine-tenths. You reproach us, therefore, with intending to do away with a form of property, the necessary condition for whose existence is the non-existence of any property for the immense majority of society.

In a word, you reproach us with intending to do away with your property. Precisely so; that is just what we intend.

From the moment when labour can no longer be converted into capital, money, or rent—into a social power capable of being monopolized—i.e., from the moment when individual property can no longer be transformed into bourgeois property, into capital; from that moment, you say, individuality vanishes.

You must, therefore, confess that by "individual" you mean no other person than the bourgeois, than the middle class owner of property. This person must, indeed, be swept out of the way and made impossible.

Communism deprives no man of the power to appropriate the products of society; all that it does is to deprive him of the power to subjugate the labour of others by means of such appropriation. . . .

The Communists are further reproached with desiring to abolish countries and nationality.

The workingmen have no country. We cannot take from them what they have not got. Since the proletariat must first of all acquire political supremacy, must rise to be the leading class of the nation, must constitute itself *the* nation, it is, so far, itself national, though not in the bourgeois sense of the word.

National differences and antagonisms between peoples are vanishing gradually from day to day, owing to the development of the bourgeoisie, to freedom of commerce, to the world market, to uniformity in the mode of production and in the conditions of life corresponding thereto.

The supremacy of the proletariat will cause them to vanish still faster. United action, of the leading civilized countries at least, is one of the first conditions for the emancipation of the proletariat.

In proportion as the exploitation of one individual by another is put an end to, the exploitation of one nation by another will also be put an end to. In proportion as the antagonism between classes within the nation vanishes, the hostility of one nation to another will come to an end. . . .

A Ten-Step Program

We have seen above that the first step in the revolution by the working class is to raise the proletariat to the position of ruling class, to establish democracy.

The proletariat will use its political supremacy to wrest by degrees all capital from the bourgeoisie, to centralize all instruments of production in the hands of the state, i.e., of the proletariat organized as the ruling class, and to increase the total of productive forces as rapidly as possible. . . .

In the most advanced countries the following will be pretty generally applicable:

1. Abolition of property in land and application of all rents of land to public purposes.

2. A heavy progressive or graduated income tax.

3. Abolition of all right of inheritance.

4. Confiscation of the property of all emigrants and rebels.

5. Centralization of credit in the hands of the state by means of a national bank with state capital and an exclusive monopoly.

6. Centralization of the means of communication and transport in the hands of the state.

7. Extension of factories and instruments of production owned by the state; the bringing into cultivation of waste lands, and the improvement of the soil generally in accordance with a common plan.

8. Equal obligation of all to work. Establishment of industrial armies, especially for agriculture.

9. Combination of agriculture with manufacturing industries; gradual abolition of the distinction between town and country by a more equable distribution of the population over the country.

10. Free education for all children in public schools. Abolition of child factory labour in its present form. Combination of education with industrial production, etc. . . .

The Communists disdain to conceal their views and aims. They openly declare that their ends can be attained only by the forcible overthrow of all existing social conditions. Let the ruling classes tremble at a Communist revolution. The proletarians have nothing to lose but their chains. They have a world to win.

Workingmen of all countries, unite!

GOLD FEVER HITS CALIFORNIA

WALTER COLTON

When gold was discovered in California in 1848, barely three months after it became a state, the largely unpopulated region was quickly inundated with people from all over the world seeking their fortunes in the gold fields. U.S. Navy chaplain Walter Colton, living in the once-sleepy town of Monterey, records how his town was affected during the course of several months after gold fever infected the local populace.

Monday, May 29 [1848]. Our town was startled out of its quiet dreams to-day by the announcement that gold had been discovered on the American Fork. The men wondered and talked, and the women too; but neither believed. The sibyls [Native American sorceresses] were less skeptical; they said the moon had, for several nights, appeared not more than a cable's length [720 feet] from the earth; that a white raven had been seen playing with an infant; and that an owl had rung the church bells.

Monday, June 5. Another report reached us this morning from the American Fork. The rumor ran that several workmen, while excavating for a millrace, had thrown up little shining scales of a yellow ore that proved to be gold; that an old Sonoranian [Mexican], who had spent his life in gold mines, pronounced it the genuine thing. Still the public incredulity remained, save here and there a glimmer of faith, like the flash of a fire-fly at night. One good old lady, however, declared that she had been dreaming of gold every night for several weeks, and that it had so frustrated her simple household economy that she had relieved her conscience by confessing to her priest—

Absolve me, father, of that sinful dream.

Tuesday, June 6. Being troubled with the golden dream almost as much as the good lady, I determined to put an end to the suspense, and dispatched a messenger this morning to the American Fork. He will have to ride, going and returning, some 400 miles, but his report will be reliable. We shall then know whether this gold is a fact or a fiction—a tangible reality on the earth, or a fanciful treasure at the base of some rainbow, retreating over hill and waterfall, to lure pursuit and disappoint hope.

GOLD FEVER

Tuesday, June 20. My messenger sent to the mines has returned with specimens of the gold; he dismounted in a sea of upturned faces. As he drew forth the yellow lumps from his pockets, and passed them around among the eager crowd, the doubts, which had lingered till now, fled. All admitted they were gold. . . . The excitement produced was intense; and many were soon busy in their hasty preparations for a departure to the mines. The family who had kept house for me caught the moving infection. Husband and wife were both packing up; the blacksmith dropped his hammer, the carpenter his plane, the mason his trowel, the farmer his sickle, the baker his loaf, and the tapster [brewer] his bottle. All were off for the mines, some on horses, some on carts, and some on crutches. . . . An American woman, who had recently established a boarding-house here, pulled up stakes and was off before her lodgers had even time to pay their bills. Debtors ran, of course. I have only a community of women left, and a gang of prisoners, with here and there a soldier, who will give his captain the slip at the first chance. I don't blame the fellow a whit; seven dollars a month, while others are making two or three hundred a day! that is too much for human nature to stand.

Saturday, July 15. The gold fever has reached every servant in Monterey; none are to be trusted in their engagement beyond a week, and as for compulsion, it is like attempting to drive fish into a net with the ocean before them. Gen. Mason, Lieut. Lanman, and myself form a mess [a group that eats together]; we have a house, and all the table furniture and culinary apparatus [necessary]; but our servants have run, one after another, till we are almost in despair: even [our servant], who we thought would stick by from laziness, if no other cause, ran last night; and this morning, for the fortieth time, we had to take to the kitchen, and cook our own breakfast. A general of the United States Army, the commander of a man-of-war . . . in a . . . kitchen grinding coffee, toasting a herring, and pealing onions! These gold mines are going to upset all the domestic arrangements of society, turning the head to the tail, and the tail to the head. . . .

Tuesday, July 18. Another bag of gold from the mines, and another spasm in the community. It was brought down by a sailor from Yuba River, and contains 136 ounces. It is the most beautiful gold that has appeared in the market; it looks like the yellow scales of the dolphin, passing through his rainbow hues at death. My carpenters, at work on the school-house, on seeing it threw down their saws and planes, shouldered their picks, and are off for the Yuba. Three seamen ran from the Warren, forfeiting their four years' pay; and a whole platoon of soldiers from the fort left only their colors [flags] behind. One old woman declared she would never again break an egg or kill a chicken, without examining yolk and gizzard [for gold flakes]. . . .

RAGS TO RICHES

Saturday, August 12. My man Bob, who is of Irish extraction, and who had been in the mines about two months, returned to Monterey four weeks since, bringing with him over $2,000, as the proceeds of his labor. Bob, while in my employ, required me to pay him every Saturday night, in gold, which he put into a little leather bag and sewed into the lining of his coat, after taking out just 12 ½ cents, his weekly allowance for tobacco. But now he took rooms and began to branch out; he had the best horses, the richest viands, and the choicest wines in the place. He never drank himself, but it filled him with delight to brim the sparkling goblet for others. I met Bob to-day, and asked him how he got on. "Oh, very well," he replied, "but I am off again for the mines." "How is that, Bob? you brought down with you over $2,000. . . ." "Oh, yes," replied Bob, ". . . but the $2,000 came easily by good luck, and has gone as easily as it came." Now Bob's story is only one of a thousand like it in California, and has a deeper philosophy in it than meets the eye. Multitudes here are none the richer for the mines. He who can shake chestnuts from an exhaustless tree won't stickle about the quantity he roasts.

Thursday, August 16. Four citizens of Monterey are just in from the gold mines on Feather River, where they worked in company with three others. They employed about thirty wild Indians, who are attached to the rancho owned by one of the party. They worked precisely seven weeks and three days, and have divided $76,844—nearly $11,000 to each. Make a dot there, and let me introduce a man, well known to me, who has worked on the Yuba River sixty-four days, and brought back, as the result of his individual labor, $5,356. Make a dot there, and let me introduce

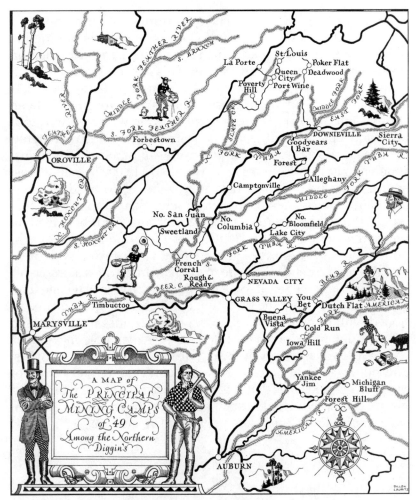

As gold fever struck thousands of hopeful prospectors, mining camps were quickly established throughout northern California.

another townsman, who has worked on the North Fork fifty-seven days, and brought back $4,534. Make a dot there, and let me introduce a boy, fourteen years of age, who has worked on the Mokelumne fifty-four days, and brought back $3,476. Make another dot there, and let me introduce a woman, of Sonoranian birth, who has worked in the dry diggings forty-six days, and brought back $2,125. Is not this enough to make a man throw down his ledger and shoulder a pick? But the deposits which yielded these harvests were now opened for the first time; they were the accumulation of ages; only the foot-prints of the elk and wild savage had passed over them. Their slumber was broken for the first time by the sturdy arms of the American emigrant.

Saturday, September 16. The gold mines are producing one good result; every creditor who has gone there is paying his debts. Claims not deemed worth a farthing are now cashed on presentation at nature's great bank. This has rendered the credit of every man here good for almost any amount. Orders for merchandise are honored which six months ago would have been thrown into the fire. There is none so poor, who has two stout arms and a pickaxe left, but he can empty any store in Monterey. . . . I met a man to-day from the mines in patched buckskins, rough as a badger from his hole, who had $15,000 in yellow dust swung at his back. Talk to him of brooches, gold-headed canes, and Carpenter's coats! Why he can unpack a lump of gold that would throw all Chesnut-street into spasms. And there is more where this came from. *His* rights in the great domain are equal to yours, and his prospects of getting it out vastly better. With these advantages, he bends the knee to no man, but strides along in his buckskins, a lord of earth by a higher prescriptive privilege than what emanates from the partiality of kings. His patent is medallioned with rivers which roll over golden sands, and embossed with mountains which have lifted for ages their golden coronets to heaven. Clear out of the way with your crests, and crowns, and pedigree trees, and let this democrat pass. Every drop of blood in his veins tells that it flows from a great heart, which God has made and which man shall never enslave. Such are the genuine sons of California; such may they live and die.

CHRONOLOGY

1775

On April 19, a column of British soldiers on a mission to collect arms in Lexington, Massachusetts, are attacked by the patriot militia in the first battle of the Revolutionary War.

1776

On July 4 the Declaration of Independence is signed in Philadelphia, claiming American independence from British rule; Adam Smith publishes *An Inquiry into the Nature and Causes of the Wealth of Nations,* a book on economics that would have a profound influence on business theory for centuries to come.

1778

The French join the Revolutionary cause and supply desperately needed money and troops to aid American independence.

1783

On September 3, the Treaty of Paris, negotiated by John Jay and Benjamin Franklin, is ratified. This treaty secures British recognition of American independence.

1787

The Constitutional Convention meets in Philadelphia to write the U.S. Constitution.

1789

A riot by hungry peasants at the Bastille Prison in Paris touches off the French Revolution.

1790

The U.S. Constitution is fully ratified by all thirteen colonies.

1791

Toussaint l'Ouverture leads a slave revolt against the French in Haiti.

1792

Austrian and Prussian allies invade France in an unsuccessful attempt to help French King Louis XVI regain his throne; Denmark is the first nation to abolish the slave trade.

1793

After being convicted for treason for his part in the Austrian invasion, Louis XVI is executed by guillotine on January 21.

1793–1794

Approximately 35,000 people are executed for trumped up charges of treason during the French Reign of Terror; Maximilien Robespierre, leader of the Reign of Terror, is himself guillotined on July 28.

1796

Edward Jenner gives the first vaccination against smallpox.

1798

English economist Thomas Robert Malthus anonymously publishes *An Essay on the Principle of Population, as It Affects the Future Improvement of Society,* a book that states that the earth is not capable of supporting the needs of the exploding eighteenth-century population.

1799–1805

Poet William Wordsworth writes several of his finest lyrical verses, the "Lucy" poems, and begins *The Prelude,* an introspective account of his own development completed in 1805.

1799

Discovery of the Rosetta Stone enables Egyptian hieroglyphics to be deciphered.

1800

Italian physicist Alessandro Volta invents the first electric battery.

1801

Islamic kingdom of Sokoto is founded in West Africa.

1803

France sells the Louisiana Purchase to the United States for $15 million, doubling the size of the young nation.

1804

General Napoléon Bonaparte names himself emperor of France, officially ending the French Revolution; Meriwether Lewis and William Clark explore the northwestern United States.

1805

Napoléon's newly formed Grand Army invades Germany and Austria, destroying both the Austrian and Russian armies that had assembled to fight the French.

1806–1807

Napoléon annexes several states that make up the present-day countries of Italy and Germany, while his armies conquer Poland, defeat Prussia, and march into Spain.

1807

American Robert Fulton builds the first successful steamboat.

1811

The Luddite Rebellion begins in England as hosiery and lace workers attack and destroy new machinery that has made their jobs obsolete; under the leadership of Simón Bolívar, Venezuela becomes the first South American country to declare its independence from Spain.

1812

The War of 1812 between Great Britain and the United States begins in June; That same month, Napoléon's Grand Army attempts to conquer Russia but is thwarted by year's end because of extremely frigid winter weather.

1813–1814

Prussia, Russia, Britain, and Sweden band together and drive the Grand Army out of every country on the continent.

1814

In August, the British burn the White House, the Capitol, and other public buildings in Washington, D.C.; Francesco Goya completes two of his most important paintings, *Second of May 1808* and *Third of May 1808*, depicting brutal massacres of unarmed Spanish citizens by French soldiers;

England and the United States sign a peace treaty ending the War of 1812 in December.

1814–1815

Between September and June, kings, emperors, and viscounts from Britain, Austria, Russia, and Prussia meet at the Congress of Vienna to redraw the map of Europe and restore pre-Napoléon dynasties across the continent.

1815

In June, Napoléon is exiled to St. Helena, an isolated island in the South Atlantic, 1,200 miles off the coast of Africa; France prohibits the slave trade.

1817–1825

The Erie Canal is constructed between Lake Erie and the Hudson River allowing pack boats to travel from the Great Lakes to New York City.

1819

Spain cedes Florida to the United States.

1820

The Missouri Compromise is signed.

1821

Mexico and Peru become independent states.

1822

Liberia, West Africa is founded as a colony for freed U.S. slaves.

1823

United States issues the Monroe Doctrine, warning European nations not to recolonize the Western hemisphere.

1824

A nearly deaf Ludwig von Beethoven finishes his rousing Ninth Symphony, one of the most highly acclaimed pieces of classical music in history.

1827

Beethoven dies; the first tracks of the Baltimore & Ohio Railroad are laid down after a boisterous celebration outside Baltimore, Maryland.

1828

The Democratic Party is formed based on the concept that the common citizen should be protected against the predatory business practices of the ruling class; their candidate, Andrew Jackson, is elected president.

1830
The first passenger steam railway opens.

1833
Slavery is abolished in British colonies; the Factory Act in England forbids employment of children under age nine.

1837–1901
Great Britain is under the reign of Queen Victoria.

1835–1840
French aristocrat Alexis de Tocqueville writes *Democracy in America,* one of the earliest studies of American politics, social interaction, customs, and manners.

1835–1836
People in Texas fight a war with Mexico in order to gain independence.

1838
More than 15,000 Cherokee Indians are ordered from their homes in Georgia and forced to march on "The Trail of Tears" to a reservation in Oklahoma. Thousands die along the way.

1839–1841
Opium War between Great Britain and China results in opening the latter to greater European penetration and reveals the weakness of the Manchu dynasty.

1844
First telegraph message is transmitted by Samuel F.B. Morse in the United States.

1845
The term "manifest destiny," first published by newspaper editor John L. O'Sullivan, quickly came into widespread use to justify the white American dominance of the North American continent.

1846
Irish potato famine reaches its height, causing the deaths of more than one million persons and the emigration of several million others.

1846–1848

The Mexican-American War results in the annexation of large
western territories by the United States and the worsening
of North-South sectional tensions over the expansion of
slavery.

1848

The Second Republic in France is established, modeled on the
government founded after the 1789 revolution; inspired by
the second French revolution, a wave of rebellion sweeps
across the European continent affecting countries such as
Austria, Hungary, Croatia, and Italy; first Convention of
Women's Rights is held in Seneca, New York; the *Communist Manifesto* is written by Friedrich Engels and Karl Marx;
gold is discovered near Sacramento, California, beginning
a frenzied gold rush that attracts hundreds of thousands
of people to the area from across the globe.

Brian Bailey, *The Luddite Rebellion*. New York: New York University Press, 1998.

T.C.W. Blanning (editor), *Oxford Illustrated History of Modern Europe*. Oxford: Oxford University Press, 1996.

Russell Bourne, *Floating West*. New York: W.W. Norton Co., 1992.

Albert Sidney Britt III, *The Wars of Napoleon*. Wayne, NJ: Avery Publishing Group, Inc., 1985.

Colin G. Calloway, *The American Revolution in Indian Country*. Cambridge, England: Cambridge University Press, 1995.

Walter Colton and Michael Kowalewski (editor), *Gold Rush a Literary Exploration*. Berkeley, CA: Heyday Books, 1997.

George Constable (editor), *The Pulse of Enterprise*. Alexandria, VA: Time-Life Books, Inc., 1990.

———, *Winds of Revolution*. Alexandria, VA: Time-Life Books, Inc., 1990.

George Dangerfield, *The Era of Good Feelings*. New York: Harcourt, Brace and Co., 1952.

Conrad L. Donakowski, *A Muse for the Masses*. Chicago: University of Chicago Press, 1977.

Frank Donovan, *Mr. Monroe's Message: The Story of the Monroe Doctrine*. New York: Dodd, Mead, & Company, 1963.

Will and Ariel Durant, *The Age of Napoleon*. New York: Simon & Schuster, 1975.

Charles W. Eliot (editor), *American Historical Documents: 1000–1904*. New York: P.F. Collier & Son, 1910.

T.R. Fehrenbach, *Lone Star: A History of Texas in the Texans*. New York: Collier Books, 1968.

Jacques Godechot, *France and the Atlantic Revolution of the Eighteenth Century, 1770–1779*. New York: Free Press, 1965.

Norman A. Graebner (editor), *Manifest Destiny*. Indianapolis, IN: The Bobbs-Merrill Company, Inc., 1968.

Lewis Hanke and Jane M. Rausch (editors), *People and Issues in Latin American History: From Independence to the Present*. New York: Markus Wiener Publishing, Inc., 1992.

Sylvia L. Horwitz, *Francisco Goya: Painter of Kings and Demons*. New York: Harper and Row, Publishers, 1974.

Thomas Jefferson, *The Constitution and the Declaration of Independence*. New York: David McKay Company, Inc., 1976.

———, *Jefferson Writings*. New York: The Library of America, 1984.

Oliver Jensen, *The American Heritage History of Railroads in America*. New York: American Heritage Publishing Co., 1975.

Lester D. Langley, *The Americas in the Age of Revolution*, New York: Macmillan, 1996.

Vicente Lecuna (compiled by), *Selected Writings of Bolivar, Volume Two 1823–1830*. New York: The Colonial Press, Inc., 1951.

Paul D. Lensink, *Events That Changed the World in the Nineteenth Century*. Westport, CT: Greenwood Press, 1996.

Karl Marx and Friedrich Engels, *Great Books of the Western World: Marx*. Chicago: Encyclopedia Britannica, Inc., 1993.

Howard Mumford Jones, *Revolution & Romanticism*. Cambridge, MA: Harvard University Press, 1975.

National Archives and Records Administration, "U.S. Bill of Rights," www.nara.gov/exhall/charters/billrights/billmain.html, December 6, 1999.

Frederic Austin Ogg, *The Reign of Andrew Jackson*. New York: Yale University Press, 1919.

Ralph D. Paine, *The Fight for a Free Sea*. New York: United States Publishers Association, Inc., 1972.

Thomas Paine and Richard Emery (editor), *Selected Writings of Thomas Paine.* New York: Everybody's Vacation Publishing Co., 1945.

Theda Perdue and Michael D. Green (editors), *The Cherokee Removal: A Brief History with Documents.* Boston: Bedford Books of St. Martin's Press, 1995.

Bradford Perkins, *Prologue to War.* Berkeley, CA: University of California Press, 1968.

Cathal Póirtéir (editor), *The Great Irish Famine.* Dublin: Mercier Press, 1995.

R.W. Postgate (editor), *Revolution from 1789 to 1906.* New York: Harper Torchbooks, 1962.

Benjamin Quarles, *The Negro in the American Revolution.* New York: W.W. Norton & Co., Inc., 1961.

John Roberts, *Revolution and Improvement.* Berkeley, CA: University of California Press, 1976.

Selden Rodman, *Haiti: The Black Republic.* Old Greenwich, CT: The Devin-Adair Company, 1978.

Clinton Rossiter, *The Political Thought of the American Revolution.* New York: Harcourt, Brace & World, Inc., 1963.

Adam Smith, *An Inquiry into the Nature and Causes of the Wealth of Nations.* New York: The Modern Library, 1965.

Eric Solsten (editor), *Germany: A Country Study.* Washington, DC: Library of Congress, 1995.

Alexis de Tocqueville, *Democracy in America, Volume 2.* New York: The Colonial Press, 1899.

Mack Walker (editor), *Metternich's Europe.* New York: Walker and Company, 1968.

Russell F. Weigley, *The Age of Battles.* Bloomington: Indiana University Press, 1991.

William Wordsworth and Bruce Wilshire (editor), *Romanticism and Evolution.* New York: G.P. Putnam's Sons, 1968.

Lionel D. Wyld, *Low Bridge! Folklore and the Erie Canal.* Syracuse, NY: Syracuse University Press, 1962.

Howard Zinn, *A People's History of the United States 1492–Present.* New York: HarperCollins, 1995.

INDEX

ABOUT THE EDITOR

Stuart A. Kallen is the author of more than 150 nonfiction books for children and young adults. He has written on topics ranging from the theory of relativity to rock-and-roll history to life on the American frontier. In addition, Mr. Kallen has written award-winning children's videos and television scripts. In his spare time, Stuart A. Kallen is a singer/songwriter/guitarist in San Diego, California.